HISTORIC AMERICAN
BUILDINGS SURVEY

District of Columbia
Catalog

1974

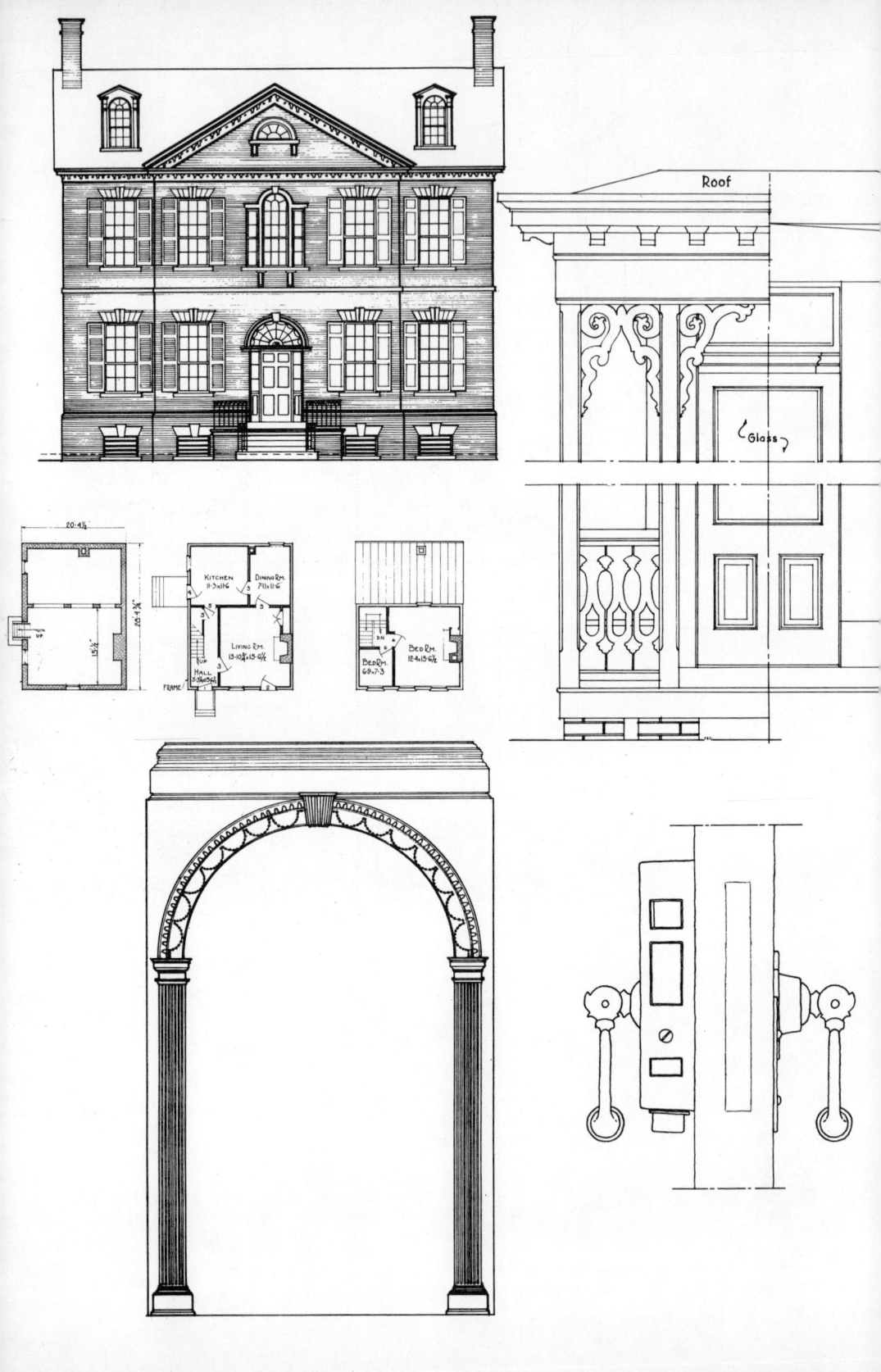

Roof

Glass

20-1½

20-4¾

15-5"

UP

FRAME

Kitchen
11-3 x 14-6

Dining Rm.
7-4 x 11-6

Living Rm.
13-10¾ x 15-6½

Hall
5-3 x 5-4

UP

DN

Bed Rm.
6-8 x 7-3

Bed Rm.
12-4 x 15-6½

Historic American Buildings Survey

National Park Service, Department of the Interior

District of Columbia Catalog

1974

Compiled by Nancy B. Schwartz

Published for the Columbia Historical Society
Washington, D.C.

by the University Press of Virginia
Charlottesville

THE UNIVERSITY PRESS OF VIRGINIA

First published 1976

Library of Congress Cataloging in Publication Data

Main entry under title:

Historic American Buildings Survey, District of
    Columbia catalog, 1974.

    Bibliography: p. xxv
    1. Architecture—Washington, D.C.—Catalogs.
2. Historic buildings—Washington, D.C.—Catalogs.
3. Washington, D.C.—Buildings—Catalogs.
I. Schwartz, Nancy B. II. Historic American Buildings
Survey. III. Columbia Historical Society, Washington,
D.C. IV. Title: District of Columbia catalog, 1974.
NA735.W3H57   917.53'04'4   75-9696   ISBN 0-8139-0618-0

Printed in the United States of America

Contents

Foreword

Since its founding as the historical society of the Nation's capital city in 1894, the Columbia Historical Society has pursued an active publication program. Along with an extensive library and archives, this publication program reflects the Society's concern for historic preservation and for the encouragement of interpretive studies of the city's past by individuals and groups. In the forty-eight bound volumes published by the Society during these eighty years, a great quantity of information has been assembled on historic sites and structures. The comprehensive analytical index of the Society's first thirty volumes, a card catalog of its library, and various indexes to the Society's files lead the inquiring mind to precise information about these significant structures. The publication of the index to the remaining eighteen volumes (in 1975) will further simplify the search for exact historical data.

In keeping with this long tradition of sponsoring studies of Washington history, the Columbia Historical Society is pleased to be able to sponsor the *District of Columbia Catalog* of the Historic American Buildings Survey. This catalog is a guide to the Survey's documentary records for over 350 buildings—standing or demolished—in the District of Columbia. The Historic American Buildings Survey, a unit of the National Park Service, has prepared records on Washington structures for over forty years and continues to add new measured drawings, professional photographs, and written documentation to its archives in the Library of Congress each year. This documentation constitutes one of the major research collections on the history of buildings in the city. The close association between the Columbia Historical Society and the National Park Service during several decades and the opportunity for the Society to sponsor the publication of this useful catalog of the HABS collection are sources of pride for the Society's members and particularly its Board of Managers.

The catalog contains a brief description and gives the exact street location for all of the listed buildings. It can, therefore, serve as a convenient guide for visiting the structures that are still standing and should prove a useful resource for residents of the Washington metropolitan area and visitors who want to gain an intimate picture of the tangible physical reminders of persons, events, and trends significant in the history of the District of Columbia.

Illustrating the need for recognition and protection of the city's historic structures, this catalog also lists many important buildings that have been demolished since they were recorded. It is the hope of the Columbia Historical Society and the Historic American Buildings Survey that this volume will encourage interest in those recorded structures which remain so that neglect of any of them or the threat of demolition will thereby be decreased.

Homer T. Rosenberger, *President*
Columbia Historical Society

Acknowledgments

The compiler wishes to thank the staff of the Historic American Buildings Survey—particularly Chief John Poppeliers and Architectural Historian S. Allen Chambers—for their helpful suggestions and encouragement. Special thanks go to Thomas Holtz for editorial and typing assistance. The cooperation of those persons who reviewed the final manuscript—Suzanne Ganschinietz of the District of Columbia / National Capital Planning Commission Historic Preservation Office; Perry Fisher, librarian of the Columbia Historical Society; and the staff of the Commission of Fine Arts—is also gratefully acknowledged. Their comments and corrections have made this catalog a more complete and useful document.

Introduction

The Historic American Buildings Survey

The Historic American Buildings Survey (HABS) is a long-range program to assemble a national archives of American architecture. Begun in 1933 by the National Park Service in collaboration with the Library of Congress and the American Institute of Architects, the Survey represented the federal government's first major step toward the identification and preservation of historic structures. Since that time thousands of records, consisting of measured drawings, photographs, and written data, have been collected and deposited in the Survey's permanent archives in the Library of Congress. The structures selected for recording represent the full range of the American building art from the crude log cabin to the modern skyscraper and span the period between the first colonial settlements and the early twentieth century. Architectural interest and merit, as well as historical associations, are the basic criteria for the selection of buildings for the Survey.

The active recording program of the Historic American Buildings Survey was terminated at the outbreak of World War II, but recognition of the continuing value of the program led to its reactivation in 1957, and extensive recording has gone on since that time. The Survey is now a part of the Historical and Architectural Surveys Division of the Office of Archeology and Historic Preservation, where it operates in cooperation with the other historic preservation programs of the National Park Service. Cornelius W. Heine is chief of the Historical and Architectural Surveys Division and is also a vice president of the Columbia Historical Society, sponsor of this catalog. John Poppeliers, chief of the Historic American Buildings Survey, directs the national recording program.

Reproduction of Records

The Historic American Buldings Survey is one of the largest national collections of its kind in the world. It includes over

30,000 measured drawings, 45,000 photographs, and 22,000 pages of written historical and architectural data for over 16,000 buildings in the United States, Puerto Rico, and the Virgin Islands. These records may be consulted at the Library of Congress, Prints and Photographs Reading Room. Copies of any of the material in the archives may be purchased at stated prices by writing to the Library of Congress, Prints and Photographs Division, Washington, D.C. 20540. The most recent records are being temporarily held in the HABS office for editorial review; they are noted in this catalog by an asterisk. Inquiries about obtaining copies of these records should be directed to the Historic American Buildings Survey, National Park Service, Department of the Interior, Washington, D.C. 20240. When ordering reproductions, buildings should be identified by the complete historic name (e.g., U.S. Soldiers Home, Chapel) and the assigned HABS number (e.g., DC-353).

HABS Recording in the District of Columbia

The Historic American Buildings Survey archives contain documentation for 347 individual buildings and 10 neighborhoods or historic districts in Washington, D.C. This documentation includes 351 architectural measured drawings, 2,225 photographs, and 1,930 pages of written historical and descriptive data that have been collected over a period of forty-one years.

HABS was created in the depths of the Great Depression with the two-fold purpose of assembling a centralized archives of the country's fast-disappearing historic architecture and providing as many jobs as possible for unemployed architects and draftsmen. The attempt to meet these two needs produced a program of such high standards and general usefulness that it was one of the few professional programs to be continued after the depression.

The organization, funding, recording techniques, and historical emphasis of the HABS program have changed over the years, and the records for the District of Columbia reflect the changes that have taken place nationally. Organization of the Survey program began in November 1933, and funds were made available in January 1934 under the Civil Works Administration. The national program was under the general direction of a small staff in the National Park Service which determined the general criteria for recording and set the standards of accuracy and quality for the records. Recording in Washington was initially under the supervision of Major H. Brooks Price, one of the thirty-nine District Officers who administered the HABS program regionally. Major Price was succeeded by Delos H. Smith when funding for the Survey was taken over in 1936 by the Works Progress Administration. It was the duty of the District Officer to recruit architects, draftsmen, and photographers from the unemployment rolls, organize them into field teams, assign the buildings to be recorded, and approve the finished records. He was assisted in the assignment of work by a five-member advisory committee which drew up a priority list of recording projects to be undertaken. Special consideration was given to buildings threatened with demolition.

The District Officer was nominated by the local chapters of the American Institute of Architects (AIA), and most of the field team members were also members of the AIA. Although a private professional organization, the AIA has cooperated with the National Park Service in conducting the Historic American

Francis Scott Key House, c. 1896 view

Buildings Survey since its inception. A third cosponsor, the Library of Congress, receives and maintains the completed records. The library had itself taken part in some pioneering architectural recording projects and was a natural choice as the repository for the HABS collection. It was easily accessible to scholars, and reproductions could be ordered by mail from the library's Photoduplication Service, making the HABS collection available to interested persons all over the country. The requirement that all material in the archives be reproducible and the ready availability of reproductions are unique aspects of the Survey when compared to similar collections in other countries.

The first recording undertaken by HABS in Washington reflects the Survey's continuing effort to document buildings that have an uncertain future, thus assuring that a graphic record of the building is preserved if the fabric itself cannot be. The first building recorded was the Francis Scott Key House, which was measured in November 1933, even before official funding for the program had begun. Other houses recorded early in 1934 were the Hamburgh Village House, the Maury House, and the Capt. Joseph Johnson House. None of these were among the grand houses of Washington which one might assume would have headed the priority list for recording. All were typical examples of the city's earliest architecture, and all were soon to be demolished.

This principle of "preservation through documentation" explains a great deal about the composition of the HABS collection for the District of Columbia, as it does about the national collection. Of the ninety-three individual structures that had been recorded by 1965, over one-third have been demolished. A number of those that survive were, at the time of their recording, under threat of demolition. In the photographic surveys of Southeast Washington neighborhoods undertaken in 1959, twenty-two of the thirty-three buildings photographed are now gone, most the victims of highway contruction. Through the years HABS has continued to stay one step ahead of the bulldozer. Among recent examples of eleventh-hour recording are the Capital Garage, the Litchfield House, and the old Washington Loan and Trust Branch Bank.

During the 1930s the men who formed the field teams were professional architects, schooled in the Beaux Arts tradition.

Capital Garage

Great emphasis was, therefore, placed upon recording structures by means of measured drawings. These drawings were beautifully rendered in an elaborate style no longer taught in architectural schools. The quality and intricacy of the draftsmanship can be seen in the examples reproduced in this catalog. Much less emphasis was placed on photographic recording, and the photographs made during the 1930s—although interesting as historical records—are generally not of high artistic or technical quality. Written documentation also received little attention from these trained architects. Although there is an extensive written report on the archeological investigation of the Mason House ruins on Roosevelt Island, generally the written data which accompany the earliest records are sparse, if they exist at all.

At the outbreak of World War II, funding of the HABS program ceased. In 1941 a national catalog was prepared listing the results of the first nine years of recording. It listed records for sixty-one structures in the District of Columbia. Active recording was not resumed until 1957 under the Mission 66

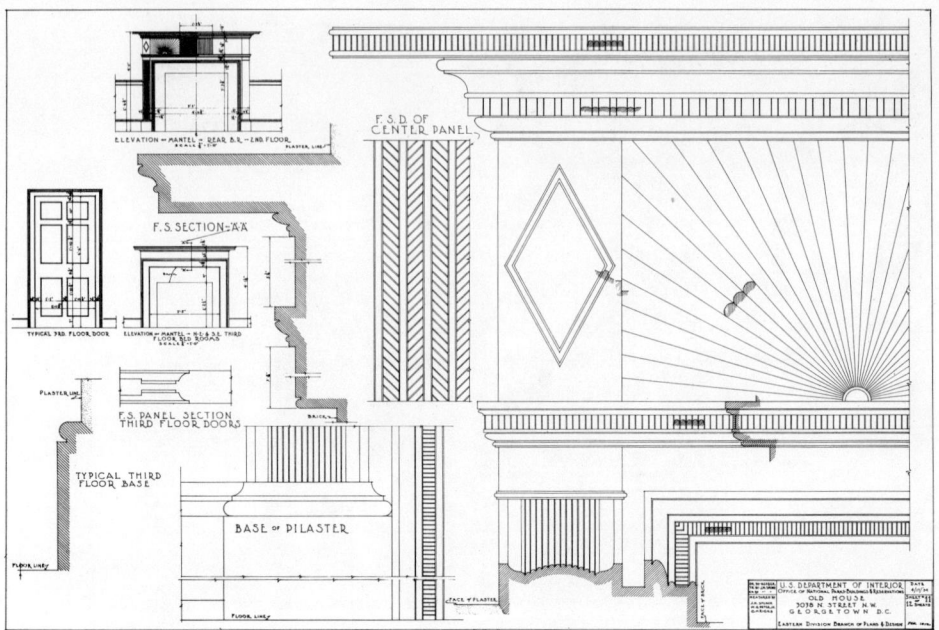

Early drawing, 1934, 3078 N. Street, N.W.

program, a ten-year plan to expand the National Park Service. In the interim the archives grew only from donations.

When the program was reactivated in 1957, economic conditions had changed drastically and professional architects were no longer available for part-time recording work. Field teams were, therefore, assembled during the university summer break and staffed with architectural students and professors from schools across the country. Students were selected on the basis of their drafting ability and, with guidance, produced admirable drawings; at the same time they gained valuable professional experience. Such student teams made measured drawings of buildings in Washington in the summers from 1962 through 1965.

More recently, emphasis has been placed on recording by means of professional photographs and written documentation to supplement the measured drawings. Since only a limited number of buildings can be recorded by the thorough and time-consuming method of hand measuring and drawing, photographic documentation of additional buildings allows far broader coverage. Heightened standards of quality now require that photographs be both archivally permanent and artistically composed for use as illustrations in publications and in educational exhibits.

In 1966 the Historic American Buildings Survey cooperated with the Commission of Fine Arts in the first of a series of six projects to record, by means of photographs and written data, the architecture of Georgetown—the early port city that became a part of the District of Columbia. These projects were undertaken by the Commission of Fine Arts as part of its responsibilities under the act which created the Old Georgetown Historic District. The earlier projects were cooperatively funded; the expenses for the later ones were assumed entirely by the Commission. Documentation from all the projects was organized in the standard HABS format, and after publication the Commission of Fine Arts donated the original records to the HABS archives, where they are available for public use. A recent Commission of Fine Arts project documenting the Beaux Arts architecture of Massachusetts Avenue has also been donated to the Survey.

A similar cooperative project, cosponsored by the Urban Design and Development Corporation, took place in 1967. Thirty buildings were documented in the Market Square area between Pennsylvania Avenue and the Old Patent Office Building, an area being considered for major redevelopment.

The Georgetown, Massachusetts Avenue, and Market Square projects contributed records for 147 Washington structures and represent the bulk of additions to the HABS archives for the city in the past ten years. Although the Survey is national in the scope of its recording activities, it has always been a relatively small program with limited funds; such donations of funds and records have insured the continued growth of the archives.

HABS also receives donations of records from individuals. Measured drawings of the Thomas Sim Lee House, the Bank of Columbia, and the Georgetown Custom House, for example, were all recent gifts from local architects. Drawings for the Oak Hill Cemetery Chapel were prepared as part of course work at the School of Design, North Carolina State University. This student program has contributed measured drawings to the HABS archives for buildings in many states.

In 1966 the eastern and western offices of HABS were

Joseph Beall House, Massachusetts Avenue Survey

combined and moved to Washington, D.C. Physical proximity has brought more Washington structures and preservation problems to the attention of the staff, and the archives have grown as a result. There has also been an effort in recent years to fill the gaps in the collection by making thorough photographic documentation of outstanding buildings—like the Octagon, the Treasury, and the Library of Congress—which had previously been left unrecorded so that limited funds could be

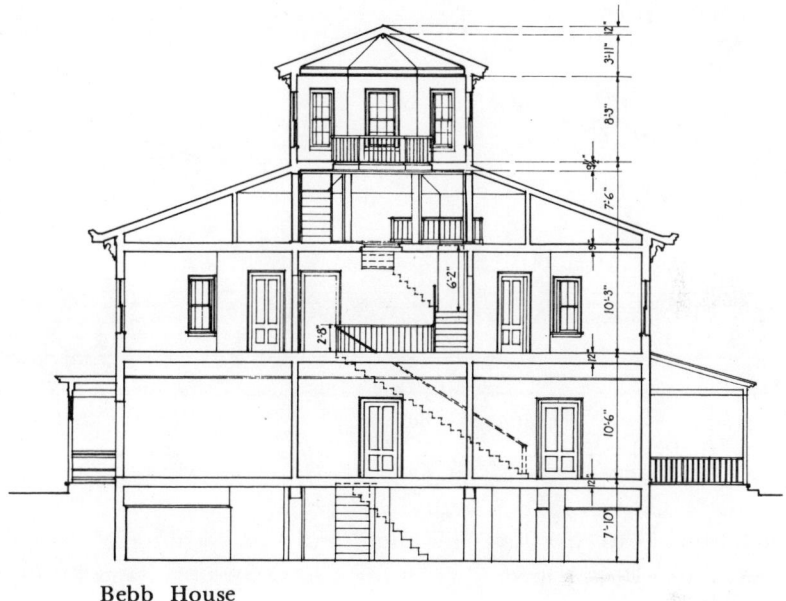

Bebb House

used to document threatened structures. Expanded recording is planned for the White House, the Supreme Court, and other major public buildings. There have also been efforts to record all National Historic Landmarks in the city and to record buildings in areas of the city that have only recently come to the attention of architectural historians, such as Logan Circle and LeDroit Park. The advanced recording technique of architectural photogrammetry has been used to document two Washington structures, the old Corcoran Gallery of Art (Renwick Gallery) and the Smithsonian Institution Building. An adaptation of aerial mapmaking techniques, architectural photogrammetry uses glass plate stereopairs and complex plotting

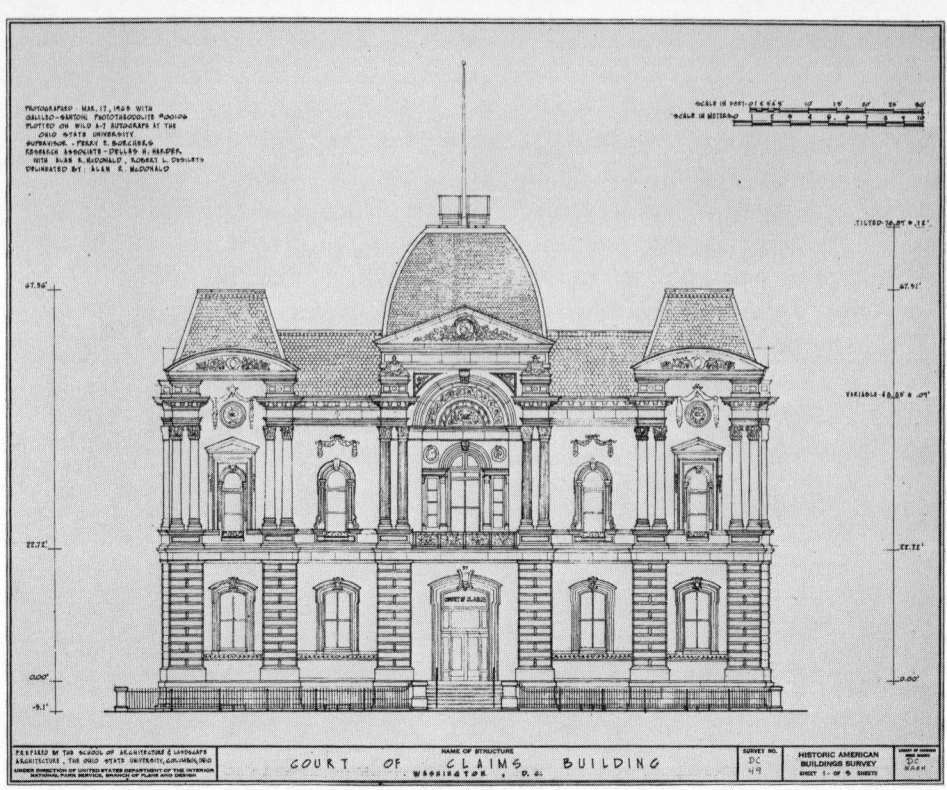

Photogrammetric drawing of the old Corcoran Gallery of Art (Renwick Gallery)

machinery to produce detailed and very accurate measured drawings. It is especially useful for recording large buildings with intricate ornamentation such as the two mentioned above.

The HABS collection for Washington, D.C., has expanded greatly since the first records were made over forty years ago. Except for the city of Phildelphia, there are more records in the HABS archives for the District of Columbia than for any other area of comparable size. However, as a perusal of this catalog will show, much work remains to be done. Some important buildings still require documentation. Others need more thorough coverage. New interests of scholars and of the community require the recording of more recently constructed structures and new building types. For instance, the Humble Service Station recorded as an example of the vanishing early gasoline stations would have been a relatively new building when the first HABS recorders were in the field concentrating on buildings of the pre–Civil War period. As funding permits, recording will continue in an effort to document the best of the city's architecture for future generations. It is hoped that this catalog will encourage the identification, documentation, and preservation of Washington's architectural patrimony.

The District of Columbia Catalog

In order to facilitate the use of the HABS collection, listings of structures recorded—and the kinds and number of records for each of the structures—have been published in catalogs from time to time. National catalogs appeared in the late 1930s and in 1941; a supplement to these was issued in 1959. The rapidly increasing size of the HABS collection has subsequently made a national catalog impractical. As a result, in 1963 the first in a new series of state and regional catalogs was published. A complete set of state and regional catalogs will be available by 1976.

This publication is a complete catalog of structures in the District of Columbia recorded by the Historic American Buildings Survey from 1933 to 1974. Each entry gives a concise description and historical account and lists the kind and number of HABS records for each documented structure. Organization of the catalog is alphabetical by historical name with cross references to current or commonly used names. Addresses have been given as accurately as possible so that the catalog may also serve as a guide for visiting the listed structures. The format for each entry is as follows: the historical name; HABS number; address; brief description, including construction material, dimensions, number· of stories, roof type, and important exterior and interior details; date of erection; architect if known; alterations and additions; important historical facts; and a listing of the number of measured drawings, photographs, photocopies of old views, and pages of written data available in the HABS archives.

Many of the buildings recorded by HABS have also been designated as city landmarks by the Joint Committee on Landmarks of the District of Columbia. This designation is noted after the appropriate entries in the catalog by the initials JCL, followed by the numerals I, II, and III, which indicate the category of significance to which the building has been assigned. Listing on the National Park Service's National Register of Historic Places (NR) and designation as a National Historic Landmark (NHL) are also noted by initials following the entries. A number of buildings in the city are protected as part of recognized historic districts; however, only structures that have been individually designated as landmarks are noted in this catalog. Historic districts in the city include Georgetown, Pennsylvania Avenue, Lafayette Square, and Massachusetts Avenue. Districts are also proposed for Capitol Hill and Anacostia.

Appended to this catalog is a listing of the Historic American Buildings Survey Inventory forms for the District of Columbia. The inventory recording program was initiated in 1953 by the American Institute of Architects, the National Trust for Historic Preservation, and the National Park Service to provide a source of basic information on buildings throughout the country upon which these organizations could draw in preservation matters. When HABS was reactivated in 1957, the inventory became an adjunct to its more comprehensive recording program. The one-page inventory forms were designed to be filled out by laymen, and most of the forms now on file are the result of voluntary efforts by interested individuals and presevation groups. Need for the inventory program declined with the expansion of the National Register of Historic Places, and it was discontinued in 1970. The forms are now on file in the Library of Congress, where they form a companion collection to the HABS records.

The following are abbreviations and symbols used in this catalog:

DC-24   Historic American Buildings Survey number. All buildings recorded by the Survey are assigned a HABS number. These numbers should be used when inquiring about a structure or ordering reproductions.

Sheets   Sheets of measured drawings.

HABSI form   Historic American Buildings Survey Inventory form. A brief one-page form on file at the Library of Congress.

JCL I, II, or III   Indicates that a building has been designated as a city landmark of Category I, II, or III by the Joint Committee on Landmarks. Category I buildings are judged to be of greatest architectural and historical significance and most worthy of preservation.

NHL   Indicates that a building has been judged to be nationally significant and has been declared a National Historic Landmark by the secretary of the interior. National Historic Landmarks are automatically listed on the National Register of Historic Places.

NR   Indicates that a building has been placed on the National Register of Historic Places maintained by the National Park Service.

ext. and int.   Exterior and interior.

n.d.   No date ascertainable.

*   An asterisk after a date indicates that the records made on that date are being temporarily held in the HABS office for editing. Inquiries about these records should be sent to the Historic American Buildings Survey, National Park Service, Department of the Interior, Washington, D.C. 20240.

Photogrammetric stereopairs   Glass plate negatives made by a special camera and used in a plotting machine to produce accurate and detailed measured drawings of buildings which are difficult to measure by hand.

Octagon House, mantel detail

1000—1002 B Street (Constitution Avenue), S.W.

Sources for the Study of Washington Architecture

For the person interested in the historic architecture of Washington, D.C., the archives of the Historic American Buildings Survey are but one source of information. The following essay is a guide to some of the publications, archival collections, and organizations that can provide information for the student of Washington architecture. It should be stated at the outset that only a few recent books approach this topic from the discipline of the architectural historian, presenting stylistic analysis and providing accurate dates and names of architects. Most publications on the buildings of the city have a more historical viewpoint, identifying significant structures not so much because they are architecturally valuable but because the people who inhabited them or the events that took place there were historically interesting. Books which represent both these approaches to historic architecture form but a small part of the literature that has been written about the District of Columbia. There are numerous histories, guidebooks, and social commentaries which may deal peripherally with architecture and from which the diligent and patient historian can glean much pertinent material—especially contemporary descriptions and illustrations. These sources of background information are so numerous that they are dealt with only briefly here. A few of the most useful examples will be discussed to illustrate the types of publications and the kinds of material that can be found in them.

Sources of Background Information

Guidebooks and Descriptive Books

Numerous books have been written over the years about Washington, D.C.—its appearance, its inhabitants, and its customs. In the introduction to his *New Guide to Washington* (Washington, D.C.: Robert Farham, 1847-48), Librarian of Congress George Watterston declares that "The Metropolis must necessarily be an object of great interest to every American, and he cannot but feel anxious to know everything concerning it."

To citizen and foreigner alike, Washington was the public face of the new nation. They looked to its physical appearance as evidence of the vitality of the new democratic form of government. As the seat of government, Washington was also the place of residence of famous men and women whose homes and life-styles were an object of constant curiosity as well as genuine historical interest. Watterston and other authors before and after him capitalized on this curiosity by producing memoirs, descriptive books, and social commentary about the city. These books can often provide important glimpses of the physical appearance and architectural development of the city.

The first guidebook to the capital appeared within thirty years of the founding of the city. William Elliot's *Washington Guide* (Washington, D.C.: S. A. Elliot, 1822) contains, among other things, one of the earliest contemporary descriptions of the Capitol Building. Two examples of descriptive books from later in the nineteenth century are *Picturesque Washington* (Providence, R.I.: J. A. and R. A. Reid, 1887) by Joseph W. Moore and *The National Capital, Past and Present* (Washington, D.C.: The Post Publishing Co., 1885) by Stilson Hutchins and Joseph W. Moore. Both contain excellent architectural plates. Particularly interesting are those which illustrate the grand Victorian houses of the West End—that exclusive residential area which grew up around Dupont Circle and whose remnants can be seen in the Blaine and Heurich mansions.

In the twentieth century *The Book of Washington* (Washington, D.C.: 1927-30), published by the Washington Board of Trade, is profusely illustrated with plates of schools, hotels, office buildings, clubs, embassies, and even factories, in addition to the usual array of government buildings and monuments. Perhaps the most complete of these descriptive guides is the noncommercial product of the Federal Writers Project, *Washington: City and Capital* (Washington, D.C.: Government Printing Office, 1937). It contains a chapter on Washington architecture, as well as tours that mention notable buildings in all parts of the city. Although probably the single most comprehensive book ever compiled about the city, and still the most valuable source, the reader must be wary of outdated material and inaccuracies. The quantity of guidebooks and descriptive books has grown steadily over the years as the number of visitors to Washington has increased. One of the better recent guides, *Washington, the New York Times Guide to the Nation's Capital* (Washington, D.C.: Robert B. Luce, 1967), also devotes a special section to the city's architecture. This essay, by noted architectural critic Ada Louise Huxtable, discusses the capital's public buildings, relating them to stylistic trends in this country and abroad.

Comprehensive Histories

Excellent background material may also be obtained from the comprehensive histories of the city that began to appear at the centenneial of the city's founding. They include the *Centennial History of the City of Washington, D.C.* (Cleveland: H. W. Crew, 1892) and William Tindall's *Standard History of the City of Washington, from a Study of Original Sources* (Knoxville, Tenn.: W. H. Crew and Co., 1914). The most useful and accurate of the large city histories is W.B. Bryan's two-volume *History of the National Capital* (New York: Macmillan, 1914). Bryan had earlier compiled for the Columbia Historical Society a *Bibliography of the District of Columbia* (Washington, D.C.: Government Printing Office, 1900), which was an impressive 200-page effort to bring together the titles of all printed matter relating to the District of Columbia. *Washington Past and Present* (New York: Lewis Historical Publishing Co., 1930), a five-volume work of history and current biography edited by John Claggett Proctor, has an essay on the city's architecture by Washington architect Appleton P. Clark, Jr. The essay covers the period from the founding of the city through the 1920s. It dwells at greatest length on buildings erected in the first third of the twentieth century, providing the original names, dates, and architects for many of the theaters, office buildings, banks, and clubs that still stand in the city.

Little was added to these standard sources until the publication of Constance McLaughlin Green's highly acclaimed volumes *Washington: Village and Capital 1800-1878*, (1962) and *Washington: Capital City 1879-1950* (1963), both published by Princeton University Press. These books present a fresh approach to urban history and are far more readable than their predecessors. They also contain extensive bibliographies and bibliographic notes to guide the reader to other sources.

Publications on the Architecture of Washington

General Publications

One of the first books to deal specifically with the domestic architecture of Washington is Mary S. Lockwood's *Historic Homes of Washington* (New York: Belford Co., 1889). Its chatty antiquarian approach and informal presentation are to be found in many subsequent publications on District buildings. Much of the book is devoted to the White House and its changing occupants, but a range of other houses is included, from David Burnes's cottage to the mid-century home of Sen. Salmon Chase.

Evidence of more serious interest in the architectural qualities of Washington buildings can be seen in the publication of measured drawings in the early twentieth century. These publications reflected a phenomenon that was occurring all across the country as architects and historians became more interested in the country's early architectural remains. Besides being the most thorough way to document a building, measured drawings provided the contemporary architect with a wealth of authentic details that he could reproduce in the Colonial Revival houses that were popular in that period. *Georgian Architecture of the District of Columbia 1750-1820* (New York: Architectural Book Publishing Co., 1914) contains drawings of seventeen Washington houses and several public buildings delineated by Harry Francis Cunningham, Joseph Arthur Younger, and Wilmer Smith. Among the buildings drawn are the Bowie-Sevier House, Saint John's Episcopal Church, the Van Ness Mausoleum, and the Old City Hall. In the 1920s the journal *Architecture* regularly featured measured drawings of historic buildings, including some from the District of Columbia. Several drawings made for this series by Albert P. Erb (October 1922 and February 1923) have been photographically reproduced in the HABS collection.

A book of continuing utility is H. Paul Caemmerer's massive volume *Washington, the National Capital* (Washington, D.C.: Government Printing Office, 1932). It deals almost entirely with the city's monumental architecture—its public buildings, largest churches, and commemorative statuary. It is the best source available on the major public buildings projects of the early twentieth century, covering not only the development of the Federal Triangle, but such mundane structures as the World War I "Tempos" and the Central Government Heating Plant. The book gives an excellent summary of the work of the various committees and commissions that were established after the turn of the century to bring about the beautification of the capital and discusses the major legislation that affected architecture and planning in the city.

Another book on the domestic architecture of the city is Harold D. Eberlein and Cortlandt V. D. Hubbard's *Historic*

Capital Garage

Houses of Georgetown and Washington City (Richmond: Dietz Press, 1958), which has been a standard, though now somewhat dated, source since its publication. The authors present a selection of sixty-one houses (including some churches), thirty-two of them in Georgetown. The houses discussed date from the earliest period of settlement, 1740-1830, and many of them, especially those outside Georgetown, have been destroyed. Although not profusely illustrated, some interesting early photographs of the houses are shown. The text deals primarily with the history of the occupants, most of whom were prominent on the national or local scene. Information was compiled largely from secondary sources, and subsequent research has revealed errors in dates and attributions. The book remains, however, the best single publication on the early domestic architecture of the city.

Only recently have books appeared which examine the entire spectrum of architecture in the city, both monumental and residential, sophisticated and vernacular. The most comprehensive of these is *A Guide to the Architecture of Washington, D.C.* (1965), published by the Metropolitan Chapter of the American Institute of Architects on the occasion of the Ninety-seventh Annual Convention of the AIA, held in Washington in 1965. The *Guide* lists and illustrates over two hundred buildings in Washington plus others in nearby Maryland and Virginia. The name, location, date of erection, and architect are given for each structure, and for most there are a few pithy lines summarizing the building's significance or appearance. The *Guide* represents the first published survey of structures in the Washington area chosen primarily for their architectural merit. Although the emphasis is on historic architecture, outstanding work by contemporary architects is also included. The first edition concentrated heavily on the central city and the residential areas of Georgetown, Capitol Hill, and Connecticut Avenue, resulting in the omission of some important, but less well-known, areas of the city such as Logan Circle, LeDroit Park, and Mount Pleasant. A revised edition (New York: McGraw-Hill, 1974), reflecting the increased knowledge of the city's architecture, corrects many of these deficiencies. A fine short essay on the architectural development of the city by Francis D. Lethbridge, Washington architect and member of the city's Joint Committee on Landmarks, precedes the pictorial survey.

In his book, *Washington Architecture 1791-1861, Problems in Development* (Washington, D.C.: U.S. Commission of Fine

Arts, 1971), Daniel Reiff traces the stylistic development of the city's architecture and examines the influence, or lack of it, of the major public buildings on the residential and commercial architecture of the city, which remained basically modest and conservative. The book is well-documented and is backed by the extensive research done over the years by the Commission of Fine Arts for whom Reiff worked. The footnotes alone contain a wealth of information on local buildings. The book represents the only extended and scholarly study of the development of the early architecture of the city that has appeared to date.

The Historic Buildings of Washington, D.C. (Pittsburgh: Ober Park Associates, 1973) by Diane Maddex illustrates and describes fifty buildings chosen by the author from the archives of the Historic American Buildings Survey. Maddex's selection shows the depth and range of the HABS collection and presents a cross section of building types in the District. Some structures, like Decatur House and Tudor Place, have long been appreciated; others are the more obscure vernacular, commercial, and institutional buildings of the city. Still others, such as the Mason House on Roosevelt Island and the McLean Mansion on McPhearson Square, have long since passed from the scene. The numerous illustrations, both photographs and measured drawings, come from the HABS collection. The book serves as a companion volume to this catalog, illustrating in depth what can only be briefly described here. There are also useful appendixes and an introduction which briefly outlines the history of efforts by federal, city, and private groups to record and preserve the city's architectural heritage.

Bibliographies

The most important guide to books and articles on American architecture is the *Bibliography of Early American Architecture* 2d ed. (Urbana: University of Illinois Press, 1968) by Frank J. Roos, Jr. This bibliography is organized by states; the section devoted to the District of Columbia contains over one hundred and sixty entries. Daniel Reiff's book, described above, has an excellent eight-page bibliography listing public documents, periodicals, and books—including a long section on nineteenth-century publications. Both of these bibliographies, however, have the limitation of listing sources that deal only with buildings erected before the Civil War. A third useful bibliography is "The Washington Bookshelf," which appeared in a special issue of the *American Institute of Architects Journal*

Chinese Community Church

entitled "Washington in Transition" (January 1963). This
annotated listing was compiled by Mary C. and Francis D. Lethbridge and presents a careful selection of publications on Washington's architecture, planning, history, and social history. The remainder of this issue of the *Journal* is devoted to a series of articles by noted architects and designers assessing the development of the capital city in the mid twentieth century. An even more thorough annotated bibliography compiled by Perry Fisher, librarian of the Columbia Historical Society, is soon to be published by George Washington University as the first in a series of quarterly monographs on the District of Columbia. The bibliography lists book-length publications on all aspects of the history of the city. It has a large section devoted to architecture, which includes a listing of biographies of some of the most prominent architects who have worked in the city. The book promises to be the most comprehensive and well-organized bibliography on the city to date. A recent publication entitled *A Bibliographic Tour of Washington, D.C.* (Washington, D.C.: Redevelopment Land Agency, 1974) is a "compilation of selected references on the architectural development of the city," compiled by Anne Llewellyn Meglis. Along with the more well-known published volumes on the city, this bibliography lists a number of obscure unpublished manuscripts and notes where they may be found. An immensely useful appendix lists the names and addresses of thirty-eight libraries and organizations which can provide architectural information about the city.

Publications of Continuing Architectural Research

The most important and thorough research to be done on Washington's architecture in recent years has been undertaken by the District of Columbia government and two federal agencies—the National Capital Planning Commission and the United States Commission of Fine Arts. In 1964 these two federal agencies—both of which have responsibilities for planning and architecture in the city—established a Joint Committee on Landmarks to conduct a city-wide survey to identify landmark districts, sites, and structures and to classify them in one of three categories according to their historical and architectural merit. Over three hundred landmarks have so far been designated. Since 1968 the Joint Committee on Landmarks has also been sponsored by the mayor of the District of

Columbia and designated by him as the District's professional review committee for purposes of making nominations to the National Register of Historic Places.

Staff support for the Joint Committee on Landmarks is provided by the joint District of Columbia / National Capital Planning Commission Historic Preservation Office. A small but extrememly competent staff conducts research on individual sites and historic districts within the city, expanding the available data on the city's architecture and enlarging the list of city landmarks. One of the primary purposes of this research is the preparation of the necessary forms to nominate District landmarks to the National Park Service's National Register of Historic Places. Listing on this register provides landmarks with a degree of protection against alteration or demolition by federally funded or licensed projects and makes available matching funds for restoration and rehabilitation. Designation as a city landmark in Categories I, II, or III, also provides important protection under a recent ordinance allowing up to a 180-day delay in demolition or alteration.

Research done by the Historic Preservation Office involves extensive use of primary source materials, such as land, deed, and tax records and building permits. The final reports represent the most thorough and accurate data yet compiled for many of the city's buildings. Unfortunately, the work of the Historic Preservation Office staff is infrequently published, but a summary of the National Register nomination forms can be found in the National Park Service publication *The National Register of Historic Places* (Washington, D.C.: Government Printing Office, 1972; *Supplement*, 1974). One of the most important aspects of the Preservation Office's work is to insure that data on historic structures is available in the initial stages of planning for urban renewal and highway or other projects which can cause large-scale destruction of the city's fabric. Two publications that serve this purpose are the *Shaw School Urban Renewal Area Landmarks* (1968) and the *Downtown Urban Renewal Area Landmarks* (1970), both published in Washington, D.C., by the National Capital Planning Commission.

The Commission of Fine Arts has been involved in the study of Washington architecture—both old and new—since it was organized in 1910. Through official reports and the individual scholarship of its staff, the Commission is responsible for more books on this subject than any other organization. Publications by H. P. Caemmerer, Daniel Reiff, and Donald Myer, all members of the Commission or its staff, are mentioned elsewhere in this essay. The Commission is concerned with the quality of public art and architecture and with the suitablility of private building adjacent to federal areas of the city. The Commission was also given architectural review powers under the act which created the Old Georgetown Historic District. To guide the Commission in exercising this authority, the staff has compiled seven excellent studies of Georgetown architecture which survey a representative sampling of buildings in the historic district. Special attention was given to areas where development and change were likely, such as the waterfront and the commercial streets. These studies were published by the Government Printing Office in limited editions between 1967 and 1970 as numbers 2, 3, 4, 5, 6, and 10 of the series entitled *Selections from the Historic American Buildings Survey.* The final study, number 10, includes a brief summary of all the previous surveys. Most of these volumes are now out of print and can be found only in library collections. However, a publication based on the survey of the waterfront area, *Georgetown Historic Waterfront: A Study of Canal and Riverside Architecture*, 2d ed. (Washington, D.C.: 1974) by Constance Werner, is currently available from the Government Printing Office. The most recent survey and publication of the Commission of Fine Arts, *Massachusetts Avenue Architecture* (Government Printing Office, 1973), deals with the Beaux Arts architecture of Embassy Row, another area subject to strong development pressures.

Washington, D.C., Architecture, Market Square (Washington, D.C.: 1969), a study similar to those described above, was published by the Urban Design and Development Corporation in cooperation with the Historic American Buildings Survey. It is a survey of the commercial and residential architecture of the Market Square area of downtown Washington, once the principal shopping area of the city. This study was published, also in a limited edition, as number 8 in the series *Selections from the Historic American Buildings Survey.*

Sections of the City

Georgetown was a thriving port city in the eighteenth century before it was incorporated into the territory set aside for the federal capital. It is today a charming and popular residential area, recognized and protected as a historic district by an act of Congress. Because it contains the largest concentration of early architecture in the city, Georgetown has been the subject of numerous publications. *Georgetown Houses of the Federal Period 1780-1830* (Cornwall, N.Y.: Architectural Book Publishing Co., Cornwall Press, 1944) by Deering Davis, Stephen P. Dorsey, and Ralph Cole Hall has an introduction that identifies the elements of the Federal style of architecture as it developed in Georgetown. The entries for individual houses, however, deal primarily with historical associations and present disappointingly little architectural analysis. The book concludes with a useful street-by-street listing of Georgetown's most important Federal style houses. Other books that deal less directly with architecture are Grace Dunlop Peter's *Portrait of Old Georgetown* (Richmond: Dietz Press, 1951), which uses old buildings to introduce interesting anecdotes about Georgetown history, and Mary Mitchell's *A Walk in Old Georgetown* (Barre, Mass.: Barre Publishers, 1966), a photographic essay that captures the atmosphere of the old town with a photographer's eye and a historian's accuracy.

The Commission of Fine Art's surveys of Georgetown have already been mentioned, as have the studies of Market Square, Massachusetts Avenue, Shaw, and the Downtown commercial area. Another study of a section of the city whose architectural qualities have only recently attracted public attention is *The Logan Circle Historic Preservation Area* (Washington, D.C.: Turner Associates, P. C. and Nicholas Satterlee and Associates, Associated Architects and Planners, 1973). This report examines the problems of protecting this remarkable residential area, preserved through neglect and now facing the threat of deterioration and commercial expansion. Besides making recommendations for zoning and restoration to preserve the nineteenth century quality of Logan Circle, the report graphically documents every building in the historic district by means of photographs and line drawings. It also discusses the historical development of the area and presents histories of some of the notable individual houses. In addition, there is a valuable essay on late-nineteenth-century building techniques and materials.

No other sections of the city have been so formally studied, although pamphlets have been produced on Cleveland Park and Capitol Hill. Evidence of increased interest in the history and architecture of such areas as LeDroit Park, Mount Pleasant, and Dupont Circle can be seen in the activities of citizens' groups and in the compiling of material for walking and bicycle tours. It is hoped that this material will find its way into print in the near future.

The Maples

Individual Buildings

Besides the more general sources already listed, a number of books and articles have been published about individual buildings in the city. The best documented structure in the city—and its single most important piece of architecture—is the United States Capitol. A monumental study of this building, still the standard reference work, is Glenn Brown's two-volume *History of the United States Capitol* (Washington, D.C.: Government Printing Office, 1899-1904). An excellent, but more concise, book dealing with the men responsible for the design, construction, and landscaping of the Capitol is *They Built the Capitol* (Richmond: Garrett and Massie, 1940) by

Ihna T. Frary. Charles Fairman's *Art and Artists of the Capitol of the United States of America* (Washington, D.C.: Government Printing Office, 1927) describes the sculpture, murals, and paintings which are a part of, or are displayed in, the Capitol. Roos's *Bibliography* lists numerous additional books and articles on the Capitol.

One would expect the White House to be equally well documented. Although many books have been written about the first families and how they decorated and furnished the house, no exhaustive study of its architecture has yet been produced. Although Roos cites a number of references, most of them are periodicals discussing one or another of the extensive renovations the house has undergone. *The White House*, rev. ed. (Washington, D.C.: White House Historical Association, 1973) illustrates a number of the original plans and reproduces drawings of possible European prototypes of the design, but the accompanying text is brief, and the bulk of the booklet is devoted to the art and decorative arts of the president's house.

The National Park Service is responsible for a number of buildings and monuments in the city. As part of its program of maintenance and interpretation, the Park Service has compiled several studies on these structures. Although not available for public purchase, copies of most of these studies can be found in public and local university libraries. They include *The Old Stone House* (1955) by Cornelius Heine (which contains a useful bibliography on the history of Georgetown),*The Frederick Douglass House* (1968) by Anna C. Toogood, and several studies by historian George Olszewski, including the *Restoration of Ford's Theater* (1963), *Construction History of Union Station* (1970), and *History of the Washington Monument* (1971).

Decatur House, historic house museum and headquarters of the National Trust for Historic Preservation, is the subject of a special issue of the quarterly magazine *Historic Preservation* (vol. 19, nos. 3 and 4, 1967). The contents are the result of the careful research upon which the interpretive program of the museum is based. The General Services Administration began a short-lived series of monographs on the buildings under its care in 1964 (Washington, D.C.: Government Printing Office). Largely the work of Donald J. Lehman, historian of the Public Buildings Service, they are accurate and well documented. Volume 1 deals with the Pension Building, Volume 2 with the Agriculture-Administration Building, and Volume 3 with the Executive Office Building. This last volume is the most extensive and was reprinted in revised form in 1970.

Tudor Place, that perfectly preserved example of the
innovative work of gentleman-architect William Thornton, is the
subject of a recent pictorial study by architectural photographer
Cervin Robinson entitled *Tudor Place, Designed by Dr. William
Thornton* (Georgetown: 1970). The book includes a "Commentary on Dr. Thornton" by Frederick D. Nichols which
reproduces Thornton's original plans for the house. It was
privately printed by Armistead Peter III, the present owner of
Tudor Place and a direct descendant of the original builder.

The feasibility study is a document, useful to architectural
historians, which has resulted from the trend to preserve
buildings through adaptive usage. Two Washington buildings
over which preservation battles have long raged are the subjects
of recent feasibility studies. In 1969 the Franklin School
Committee published the two-part study *The Franklin National
Education Center,* which gives the historical background and
architectural description of the city's most famous nineteenth
century school building. The recently released *Feasibility Study
for the Renovation of the Old Post Office* (Boston: Architectural Heritage, 1974) contains similar information for the
Romanesque Revival Post Office Building on Pennsylvania
Avenue.

Periodicals

In addition to the books discussed so far, periodicals carry
numerous informative articles on Washington architecture.
Special mention should be made of the articles and illustrations
that appear in the professional magazines of the late nineteenth
and early twentieth centuries such as *Architecture* and *Architectural Record.* The *Journal of the Society of Architectural
Historians* also occasionally carries articles on some aspect of
Washington architectural history. The best source for locating
these articles is the *Art Index* (New York: H. W. Wilson Co.),
which has indexed the contents of the major national art and
architectural journals since January 1929.

One of the richest sources of material on Washington's historic
buildings is the *Records* of the Columbia Historical Society.
Articles range from reminiscences of elderly residents to Henry
Glassie's excellent study of disappearing Victorian architecture
in the city (vol. 63-65, pp. 320-65). An article of particular
interest to students of Georgetown architecture (Vol. 63-65, pp.
386-400) describes the rediscovery in the National Archives of
the early tax assessment lists. These have allowed, for the first
time, the accurate dating of many of Georgetown's houses.

Printed indexes to the *Records* are available, and complete sets of the volumes, beginning with number 1 in 1894, are in the Columbia Historical Society's library and the Washingtoniana Room of the Martin Luther King Library.

Two series of newspaper articles written for the *Evening Star* by devoted students of Washington history contain much architectural information—particularly about those buildings that are more obscure or have been demolished. These are John Harry Shannon's "The Rambler," published between 1912 and 1927, and a similar series by John Claggett Proctor, which appeared in the *Sunday Star* from 1928 through 1949. A selection of Proctor's articles was published in a single volume, *Washington and Environs,* in 1949 ([Washington, D.C.?], n.p.). An index to "The Rambler" is in Volume 46-47 of the Columbia Historical Society *Records*. A card index to Proctor's articles is located in the Washingtoniana Room.

Books on Related Subjects

Several other books should be mentioned which deal with subjects related to architectural history. One is *Bridges and the City of Washington* by Donald B. Myer (Washington, D.C.: Commission of Fine Arts, 1974), an account of those structures—ranging from the strictly utilitarian to the grandly architectural—which have played a vital role in the plan and growth of this river-bound city. Another is *The Outdoor Sculpture of Washington, D.C.* (Washington, D.C.: Smithsonian Institution Press, 1974) by James Goode, which documents not only the city's numerous commemorative monuments, but architectural sculpture as well. A history of the city's fire department, *100 Years of Glory* (Washington, D.C.: Fire Fighters Association District of Columbia, 1971), has an appendix listing firehouses in the city, their dates, and the companies which occupied them. An equally useful appendix listing the transit-related structures in the city can be found in *100 Years of Capital Traction* (College Park, Md.: Taylor Publishing Co., 1972) by LeRoy O. King.

Washington is one of the great planned cities of the world, and that plan has affected the placement and appearance of the city's buildings. Architects have had the benefit of broad streets and long vistas designed by Maj. Pierre L'Enfant, but they have also had their ingenuity taxed by his spokelike intersections and the irregularly shaped lots that surround them. Much attention

has been given to L'Enfant's plan, especially after the McMillan
Commission revived interest in restoring its grandeur in the
early twentieth century. Roos lists numerous articles about the
plan and its creator. *L'Enfant and Washington, 1791-1792*
(Baltimore: Johns Hopkins University Press, 1929) is a collection of original manuscripts relating to L'Enfant's work
organized by Elizabeth Kite. H. Paul Caemmerer has written a
useful, if not definitive, biography of the planner, *The Life of
Pierre Charles L'Enfant, Planner of the City Beautiful* (Washington, D.C.: New Republic Publishing Co., 1950). The most
important single work on this subject is John W. Reps's
*Monumental Washington: The Planning and Development of the
Capital Center* (Princeton: Princeton University Press, 1967). It
covers not only the origins of the plan with L'Enfant, but its
expansion in the twentieth century when the McMillan Commission optimistically brought together the country's most eminent
architects, artists, and planners to create the world's most
beautiful capital.

There is even a sizable quantity of literature devoted to the
individual elements of the city's plan. The efforts to turn
Pennsylvania Avenue into a great ceremonial way have gener-
ated numerous reports, beginning with that of President
Kennedy's Temporary Commission on Pennsylvania Avenue
through the recent report of the Pennsylvania Avenue Development Corporation. The history of this famous street is more
entertainingly told by Mary Cable in *Avenue of the Presidents*
(Boston: Houghton Mifflin Co., 1969). Many of the parks and
squares of the original plan are maintained by the National Park
Service, which has compiled a series of historical studies about
them. Like previously mentioned Park Service publications, they
are generally available in local libraries. They include Joan
Stanley's report *Judiciary Square* (1968) and George Olszewski's reports *Lafayette Square* (1964), *Dupont Circle* (1967),
Farragut Square (1968), *Lincoln Park* (1968), *Franklin Park*
(1970), *Mt. Vernon Square* (1970), *The President's Park South*
(1970), and *The Mall* (1970).

Archival Collections

Aside from published works on Washington architecture, a word
should be said about the location of archival collections that
contain significant historical materials. Nearly all of the sources
discussed in this essay can be found in the collections of the

Columbia Historical Society library and the Washingtoniana Room of the Martin Luther King Library. Both libraries have long maintained useful files of newspaper clippings and pamphlets, as well as collections of old maps, plat books, and directories necessary to the study of architectural history on a local level. The Peabody Room of the Georgetown Branch of the District Public Library specializes in the history of that area of the city.

The Library of Congress is an excellent source of published materials as well as original documents. The library's Prints and Photographs Division houses the permanent archives of the Historic American Buildings Survey and the Pictorial Archives of Early American Architecture, a forerunner of HABS. Other graphic collections contain old photographs, maps, and manuscripts relating to the District. Among the library's treasures are a number of original architectural drawings, including Latrobe's beautiful watercolor renderings of Washington buildings.

Documents concerning the construction, alteration, and maintenance of the city's federal buildings can be found in the National Archives. Because of the unusual symbiosis between the city and the federal government, documents of a purely local nature can be found there as well. Mention has already been made of the Georgetown tax assessment records. Recently the District building permits—which contain important information on late-nineteenth- and twentieth-century buildings—were transferred from city jurisdiction to the archives.

The late 1960s and 1970s imprints on many of the books mentioned in this essay are an indication of how recently Wash-

Paving stones at M and Bank Streets, Georgetown

ington's historic architecture has become a topic of widespread interest to the residents of the metropolitan area. This corresponds to growing nationwide interest in the historic man-made environment which brought about the passage of the National Historic Preservation Act of 1966. Because of such interest, it is important that catalogs of the holdings of the Historic American Buildings Survey—our national archives of historic architecture—be made as widely available as possible. Only in this way can the fullest use be made of this important research collection. By making possible the publication of this catalog of the HABS records for the District of Columbia, the Columbia Historical Society continues its long tradition of serving the city by promoting the study of its history. The Historic American Buildings Survey is grateful for this cooperation.

HISTORIC AMERICAN
BUILDINGS SURVEY

District of Columbia
Catalog

1974

Adas Israel Synagogue

Adams Building (DC-214), 816 F St., N.W. Brick, 34'-8" (two-bay front) x 70', two stories, flat roof, windows in groups of three, arched brick hood molds, patterned brick frieze, corbel course, paneled wooden cornice with brackets. Built 1878; storefront and interior remodeled. 3 ext. photos (1969); 5 data pages (1969). NR, JCL II

Adams, Henry, Mansion (doorway). See House (DC-299), 2618 30th St., N.W.

Adams-Mason House (DC-161), 1072 Thomas Jefferson St., N.W. (Georgetown). Frame with clapboarding, rear brick ell, 20'-5" (three-bay front) x 67', two-and-a-half stories, gable roof, side hall plan, simple wooden mantels. Built c. 1810. 3 ext. photos (1967), 4 int. photos (1967), 1 ext. photocopy (c. 1899), 1 copy of sketch plans (1967); 11 data pages (1967). JCL III

Adams Memorial (popularly known as *Grief*) (DC-280), In section E, Rock Creek Cemetery, entrance at Webster St. and Rock Creek Church Rd., N.W. Heavily shrouded cast bronze figure seated on a rough stone and backed by a monolithic slab of polished granite, stone bench faces monument, site screened by foliage from rest of cemetery. Erected 1891 by Henry Adams as a memorial to his wife, a suicide; Augustus Saint-Gaudens, sculptor; Stanford White designed setting. 7 ext. photos (1974*). NR, JCL II

Adas Israel Synagogue (DC-173), originally at SE. corner 6th and G Sts., N.W., moved to NE. corner 3d and G Sts., N.W. Brick, 25' (three-bay front) x 62'-4", two stories, gable roof with cylindrical cupola, tall narrow windows with louvered fans and brick hoods, semicircular projection from rear wall contains ark, sanctuary on upper floor with women's gallery across rear, pedimented enframement around doors to ark. Built 1873-76; Max Kleinman, draftsman; moved to present site in 1969 when threatened by demolition; to be restored as a museum. Oldest synagogue building in Washington. Congregation split from Washington Hebrew Congregation in 1869 over issue of reform movement. 5 sheets (1968*, including plan, elevations, sections); 2 ext. photos (1969*), 2 int. photos (1969*), 1 photocopy of building being moved (1969*); 7 data pages (1969*). NR, JCL II

Aged Women's Home. See John Lutz House (DC-105), 1255 Wisconsin Ave., N.W. (Georgetown).

Alexander Graham Bell Association for the Deaf. See Volta Bureau (DC-245), 1537 35th St., N.W. (Georgetown).

American Bank Building (DC-305), 1315-17 F St., N.W. Brick with rusticated ashlar facing, approx. 51' (three-bay facade), seven stories plus story-and-a-half behind mansard roof, rear portion behind lightwell has convex copper mansard, two five-story oriel windows terminate in gabled dormers, arcaded treatment on lower two floors, Romanesque Revival style. Built 1886; A. B. Mullett and Co., architects; tower removed, shop front altered. 1 ext. photo (1967*).

American Institute of Architects Headquarters. See The Octagon (DC-25), 1799 New York Ave., N.W.

American Institute of Architects Library. See The Octagon Stable (DC-336), rear of 1799 New York Ave., N.W.

Anderson, Larz, House (Society of the Cincinnati Headquarters) (DC-255), 2118 Massachusetts Ave., N.W. Brick over partial steel frame, limestone veneer, first floor rusticated, H-shaped with projecting wings on N. joined by a screen wall to form a forecourt, 137'-8' (wings are 30' wide and project 40') x 106', three stories with basement and attic, slate mansard roof, N. facade dominated by two-story semicircular Composite entrance portico, S. facade has one-story loggia between wings, late Renaissance Revival style, interior contains 50 rooms, public rooms on first and second floors, bedrooms above, two-story central ballroom, rooms finished in variety of ornate and eclectic revival styles. Built 1902-5 by Little and Browne, architects, for Larz Anderson III, minister to Belgium in 1911 and ambassador to Japan in 1912. A fine example of early 20th C. eclecticism. Became headquarters of Society of the Cincinnati in 1939. Some of rooms altered for gallery use, but house

and furnishings basically unaltered. 3 ext. photos (1971*), 5
int. photocopies (n.d.*), 3 photocopies of drawings (1902*,
1938*); 27 data pages (1970-73*). NR, JCL II.

Apartment House (DC-227), 507 6th St., N.W. Brick, 42′ front
(five bays), four stories above basement, flat roof, limestone
trim, patterned tile frieze, elaborate corbeled cornice, central
hall. Probably built c. 1870. 1 ext. photo (1969); 1 data page
(1969).

Apex Liquor Store. See Central National Bank Building
(DC-229), 633 Pennsylvania Ave. at C and 7th Sts., N.W.

Argyle Terrace. See Miller House (DC-275), 2201 Massachusetts
Ave., N.W.

Army Medical Museum and Library (DC-306), N.W. corner 7th
St. and Independence Ave., S.W. Brick with terra-cotta trim,
U-shaped with small two-story wing in center of U, nineteen-
bay front, eleven-bay flank, three stories on raised basement,
gable roof on central portion, hipped roofs with monitors on
wings, arcaded fenestration, four-story central gabled entrance
pavilion, corbeled cornice, two-story exhibit galleries with
exposed iron-truss roofs. Built 1886; demolished 1969. Housed
collection of surgical and medical specimens established in 1862
to help reduce loss of life and limbs in combat. Collection
moved to new location. 5 ext. photos (1969*), 4 int. photos
(1969*). NHL(collection only)

Army War College (National War College) (DC-277), in Fort
Leslie J. McNair, entrance on P St. between 3d and 4th Sts.,
S.W. On Greenleaf Point overlooking confluence of Potomac
River, Washington Channel, and Anacostia River. Brick with
granite trim, cross-shaped with very short cross arms, three
stories, terrace on N., basement exposed on S., cross gable roof
with acroteria, dome at crossing, principal entrance and E. and
W. gable ends have distyle *in antis* porticoes with great arches
above the entablature containing sculpted eagles, on S. elevation
central feature is two-story bow, third story treated as
clerestory with arched openings, Classical Revival style, central
three-story rotunda with balustraded galleries, entire W. wing
contains library, E. wing offices and classrooms. Built 1903-7;
McKim, Mead and White, architects. Army War College established as part of Theodore Roosevelt and Secretary of War

Army War College

Elihu Root's efforts to modernize the U.S. army after Spanish-American War. Provided officer education and centralized planning and coordination. After W.W. II became National War College serving same function for all branches of the military. 6 ext. photos (1974*), 5 int. photos (1974*). NHL, JCL II

Arts Club of Washington. See Timothy Caldwell House (DC-84), 2017 I St., N.W.

Atlas Building. See Warder Building (DC-216), 527 9th St., N.W., SE. corner 9th and F Sts., N.W.

Australian Embassy (former). See Wilkins House (DC-276), 1700 Massachusetts Ave., N.W.

Bank of Columbia (later Georgetown Town Hall and District of Columbia Engine Company No. 5 Firehouse, now National Firefighting Museum) (DC-119), 3210 M St., N.W. (Georgetown). Brick, 38'-10" (four uneven bays) x approx. 80' (including one-story rear kitchen and horse area addition), three stories, flat roof, corbeled cornice, brick belt courses, two vehicular doors and a pedestrian door on first floor, interior completely altered, stable at rear of lot. Built 1796 to house Bank of Columbia, the city's second bank; headquarters for Bureau of Indian Trade 1807-22; Georgetown Town Hall and Mayor's Office 1823-58; converted to firehouse 1883, served that function until 1940. 6 sheets (1973*, including plans, elevations, section, one sheet of stables); 1 ext. photo (1966); 5 data pages (1966); HABSI forms (1959, 1960). NR, JCL II

Barber Shop (DC-121), 3251 M St., N.W. (Georgetown). Brick, approx. 10' (two-bay front) x 35', two stories, flat roof, wooden shop front, round-arched windows on second floor, stamped metal cornice. Built c. 1887-90. 1 ext. photo (1966), 1 int. photo (1966); 6 data pages (1966).

Barney, A. Clifford, House. See Charles Evans Hughes House (DC-278), 2223 R St., N.W.

Barney, Alice P., Studio (DC-256), 2306 Massachusetts Ave., N.W. on Sheridan Circle. Brick, stuccoed on facade, ashlar-faced on first floor, 33' (three-bay front) x 60'-6", four-and-a-half stories, tile mansard roof, shaped front parapet, third-floor studio in late medieval style has large fireplace with gallery above, beamed ceiling. Built 1902; Waddy B. Wood, architect; garage and garden wall added 1911. Designed as private cultural center and studio for artist Alice P. Barney. 1 ext. photo (1970*), photocopy of original drawing (1902*); 3 data pages (1970-73*).

Barney Neighborhood House. See Duncanson-Cranch House (DC-128), 468-70 N St., S.W.

Barney's Restaurant. See Brown's Marble Hotel (DC-322), 621 Pennsylvania Ave., N.W.

Barrett, James I., House (DC-180), 1400 29th St., N.W. (Georgetown). Brick, 36'-9" (three-bay front) x 32'-8", two stories, flat roof, bracketed wooden cornice, main entrance in central bay has pediment on scroll brackets, east facade has five paired windows with cast-iron hoods, central hall plan. Built c. 1867. Home of Julius A. Krug, secretary of the interior 1946-49. 1 ext. photo (1968), photocopy of sketch plan (1968); 11 data pages (1968, 1969).

Bassin's Restaurant. See Commercial Building (DC-313), 1347 Pennsylvania Ave., N.W.

Beale, Joseph, House (now Embassy of the Arab Republic of Egypt) (DC-257), 2301 Massachusetts Ave., N.W. at intersection of Massachusetts Ave., R St., and Sheridan Circle, N.W. Stuccoed brick with limestone trim, 68'-10" (three-bay convex Sheridan Circle facade) x 55'-4", four stories, flat roof, paneled parapet, rusticated ground floor, corner quoins at second and third floors, Venetian loggia in central bay of second floor, Roman Revival style, very ornate plasterwork, especially in circular second floor sitting room. Built 1907-9; Glenn Brown, architect. 3 ext. photos (1970*, 1971*), 8 int. photos (1971*), 2 photocopies of original drawings (1907*), photocopy of plan (1973*); 15 data pages (1970-73*). NR, JCL II

Beall's Express Building (DC-80), 1522 Wisconsin Ave., N.W. (Georgetown). Brick, three-and-a-half stories, gable roof with end parapet, dormers, dogtooth cornice, arched areaway. Built early 19th C.; alterations. 1 ext. photo (1959). JCL III

Bebb House (Octagonal House) (DC-13), 1830 Phelps Pl., N.W. at end of Le Roy Pl., N.W. Frame octagon, originally stuccoed,

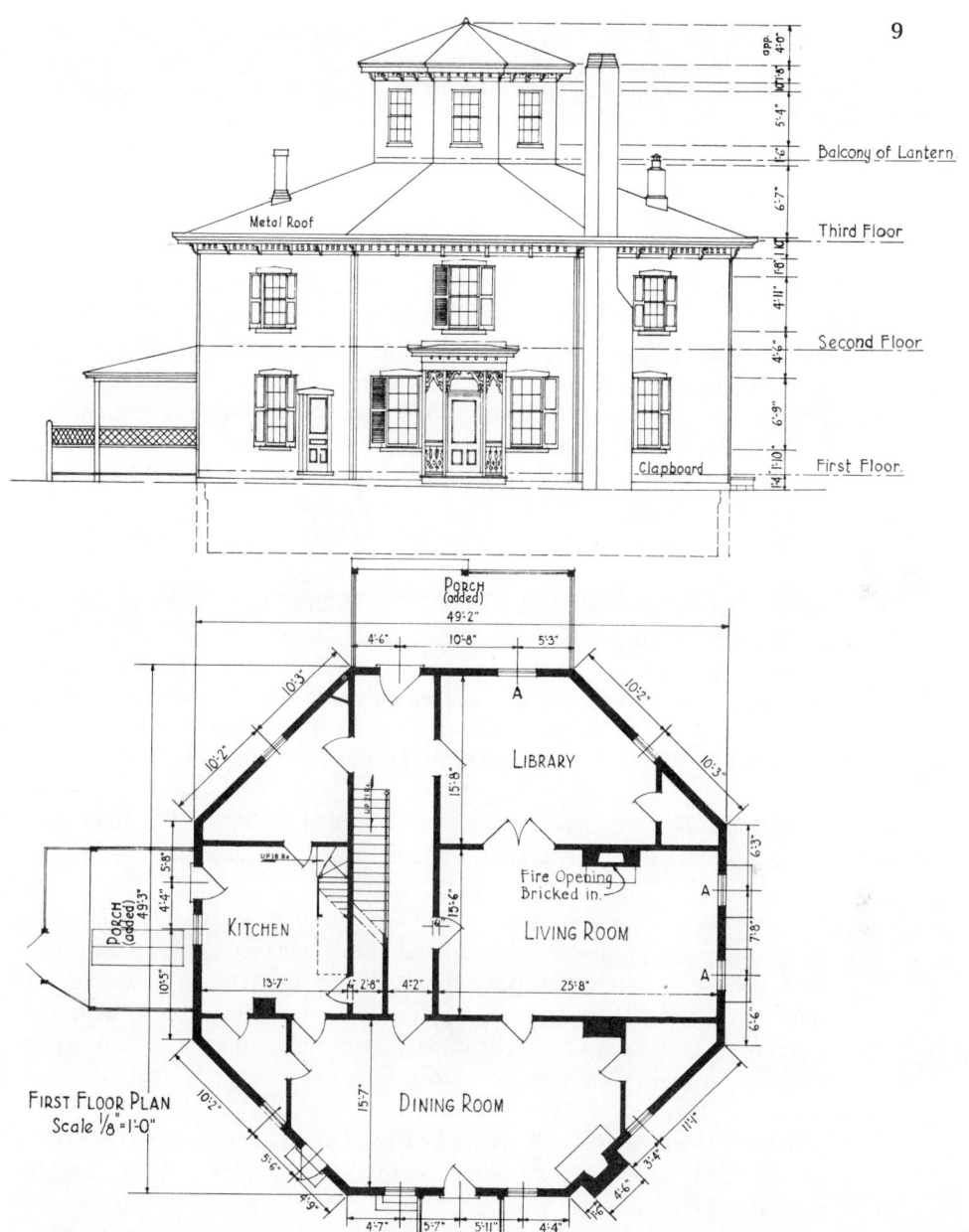

Balcony of Lantern.

Third Floor

Second Floor

First Floor.

Metal Roof

Clapboard

app. 4'-0"
10'-5½"
5'-4"
7'-0"
6'-7"
10'-6½"
4'-11"
4'-6"
6'-9"
1'-0"
4'-10"

Porch
(added)
49'-2"

4'-6"   10'-8"   5'-3"

A

10'-3"   10'-2"

10'-2"   10'-3"

LIBRARY

15'-8"

6'-3"

UP 18 Rs.

Fire Opening
Bricked in.   A   7'-8"

KITCHEN   15'-6"   LIVING ROOM

Porch
(added)
49'-3"

5'-8"
4'-4"
10'-5"

13'-7"   2'-6" 4'-2"   25'-8"   A   6'-6"

15'-7"

DINING ROOM

10'-2"

5'-6"

4'-9"

4'-7"   5'-7" 5'-11"   4'-4"   1'-6"   4'-6"   3'-4"   11'-1"

FIRST FLOOR PLAN
Scale ⅛"=1'-0"

Bebb House

later clapboarded, 49'-2" x 49'-2" (approx. 20'-5" per side), two stories, hipped roof with central cupola, bracketed cornice. Built 1865; demolished 1949. 2 sheets (1936, including plans, elevation, section, details).

Bellevue. See Dumbarton House (DC-10), 2715 Q St., N.W. (Georgetown).

Berry, Philip T., House (DC-253), 1402 31st St., N.W. (Georgetown). Frame, 40' (three-bay front) x 33', 25' x 20' ell to west, two-and-a-half story main block, two-story ell, mansard roof with dormers, cornice with paired brackets, central hall plan, pierced plaster molding and ceiling medallions in drawing room. Built c. 1865; present one-story porch is old but not original to house; it replaced two-story piazza added in late 19th C.; garage and pantry built 1925; interior remodeled 1953. 4 ext. photos (1968, 1969), 3 int. photos (1969); 14 data pages (1969).

Birch Funeral Home (DC-142), 3034 M St., N.W. (Georgetown). Brick, rectangular, 26'-6" (three-bay front) x 45'-3", three stories, low gabled roof, cast-iron hood molds, pressed metal cornice, two-story brick stable behind, now converted to a garage. Built c. 1866; first floor front and interior altered. 3 ext. photos (1967); 9 data pages (1967).

Birch, W. Taylor, House (DC-187), 3099 Q St., N.W. (Georgetown). Brick with brownstone trim, irregular plan, 35' (31st St. facade) x 50' (Q St. facade), three stories with raised basement, hipped roof, circular tower at SW. corner with conical roof, projecting polygonal bay at SE. corner has second-story balcony and flat roof with parapet, rough-faced brownstone facing on basement extending to second floor level on tower and at main entrance, tall paneled chimney, Richardsonian Romanesque details, interior has paneled staircase, wainscoting, and original mantels. Built c. 1888; Thomas F. Schneider, architect. 2 ext. photos (1968, 1969), 4 int. photos (1968), 2 ext. photocopies (c. 1928), photocopy of sketch plan (1968); 11 data pages(1968).

Blair House. See Joseph Lovell House (DC-45), 1651 Pennsylvania Ave., N.W.

Bodisco House. See Clement Smith House (DC-174), 3322 O St., N.W. (Georgetown).

Bomford's Mill (now Wilkins-Rogers Milling Company)
(DC-143), SW. corner of Potomac and Grace Sts., N.W.
(Georgetown). Brick, 40'-2" (two-bay front) x 129'-6" (12
bays), four stories with fully exposed basement on south,
millrace tunnels beneath, flat roof, open plan. Built 1845 by
Col. George Bomford as a cotton mill, converted to a flour mill
in 1866, altered 1883 and 1932. Only old mill remaining along
C & O Canal in Georgetown. 3 ext. photos (1967), 12 int.
photos (1967), 1 photocopy of plate (1886), 2 sketch plans
(1967); 15 data pages (1967). JCL II

Bowie-Sevier House (now Episcopal Church Home) (DC-60),
3124 Q St., N.W. (Georgetown). Brick, original house has
five-bay facade, two-and-a-half stories, basement exposed on S.,
gable roof, central hall plan, cornice with paired modillions,
one-story three-bay wooden porch on S. (garden) facade, that
facade also has fanlighted door and round-headed window in
central sunken bay. Built c. 1805 by shipping merchant
Washington Bowie; wings added after 1890 by owner John
Sevier; further additions and alteration 1957 when converted to
Episcopal Church Home, Horace Peaslee, architect; now a
five-part plan with two-story hyphens and wings. 2 ext. photos
(1942). JCL II

Brady, Mathew, Studio. See Gilman's Drug Store (DC-129), 627
Pennsylvania Ave., N.W.

Brickyard Hill House (DC-158), 3134 South St., N.W. (Georgetown). Frame with clapboarding, eastern half of double house,
14'-6" x 33'-7" (three bays), two stories, eastern half of gable
roof covers this house, side entrance, original wooden mantels.
Built c. 1800, probably by Robert Peter. 3 ext. photos (1967),
5 int. photos (1967); 13 data pages (1967). JCL III

Bronaugh-Bibb-Libbey House (DC-209), 1408 35th St., N.W.
(Georgetown). Frame row house, 24' (three-bay front) x 26',
23' x 30' rear addition, two-and-a-half stories on raised
basement, mansard roof with dormers, bracketed modillion
cornice, modillion entablature on heavy scrolls above entrance,
side hall plan. Built c. 1865; rear portion may be 1817 house
which originally stood on lot; interiors altered. Home of George
M. Bibb, secretary of the treasury under President Tyler. 1 ext.
photo (1968*); 19 data pages (1968*).

Brickyard Hill House .

Brown House (DC-191), 1404 35th St., N.W. (Georgetown). Stuccoed brick, approx. 20′ (three-bay front) x 30′ (not including rear two-story addition), two-and-a-half stories on fully exposed basement, gable roof, granite stoop and curving granite stairs with wrought-iron railing, recessed entrance with classical surround of pilasters and entablature, side hall plan. Built 1791 for Dr. William Brown, surgeon-general in the Revolutionary War and author of first American pharmacopia. Later home of George M. Bibb, secretary of the treasury under President Tyler. 1 ext. photo (1968*); 21 data pages (1968*).

Brown's Marble Hotel (formerly Indian Queen Hotel, later Metropolitan Hotel, now Barney's Restaurant) (DC-322), 621 Pennsylvania Ave., N.W. Present fragment is a two-bay two-story portion of SW. corner of original building, first floor commercial front, second floor has marble facing, tall windows with flanking pilasters, entablature, cornice and antefix. First hotel built on site c. 1804; by 1832 site occupied by a four-and-a-half story gabled structure with lower symmetrical wings; marble front added probably c. 1851 by second owner, Jesse Brown, who made building a five-story, approx. twenty-bay structure with balustraded flat roof; all demolished 1932 except SW. fragment. Popular early Washington hostelry; Tyler sworn in as president in one of parlors. 1 ext. photo (1967*).

Buehler-Sullivan House (DC-189), 3617 O St., N.W. (Georgetown). Frame row house, L-shaped, approx. 16′ (two-bay front) x 35′, two stories, gable roof, wide original weatherboarding on W. side. Probably built between 1842 and 1850; little altered. 1 ext. photo (1968*); 14 data pages (1968*).

Building (DC-228), 625 E St., N.W. Sandstone and brick, about 20′ front (three bays), four stories, gable roof, second-story rusticated arcade with pedimented windows, upper stories smooth ashlar, windows with rope molding trim, large wooden cornice with console brackets. Probably built during the 1850s either as residence or combined shop and residence; ground story remodeled. 1 ext. photo (1969); 1 data page (1969).

Bussard-Newman House (DC-196), 1311 35th St., N.W. (Georgetown). Frame, 21′ (three-bay front) x 35′, two-and-a-half stories, gable roof, side hall plan. Built between 1805 and 1808 by Daniel Bussard; interior extensively altered. 1 ext. photo (1968*); 16 data pages (1968*).

Cairo Hotel (DC-307), 1615 Q St., N.W. Brick with stone trim, eleven bays x six bays, twelve stories, flat roof which originally had roof garden, wide overhanging metal cornice, rusticated stone facing on first three floors and entrance, massive entrance arch of Romanesque character, polygonal bays, decorative balconies, stone belt courses, low-relief arabesque detail in the "East Indian" manner. Built 1894; Thomas F. Schneider, architect; being remodeled as apartments 1973-74, Arthur Cotton Moore, architect. Tallest private building in the city. Its 165′ height led to imposition of height restrictions in 1910. 2 ext. photos (1970*), 2 int. photos (1970*).

Caldwell, Elias B., House (DC-137), 206 Pennsylvania Ave., S.E. One unit of double house, brick, four-bay front, three stories, gable roof, splayed lintels with keystones, elliptical fanlight and side lights, hall arch with fluted pilasters. Built c. 1810;

Cairo Hotel

Supreme Court met here after Capitol burned by British; demolished. 2 photocopies of measured drawings (c. 1924*, including entrance and hall arch).

Caldwell, Timothy, House (now Arts Club of Washington) (DC-84), 2017 I St., N.W. Brick, L-shaped, 32'-5" (four-bay front) x approx. 73', three-and-a-half stories, gable roof, entrance with side lights and elliptical fanlight, stone window lintels of splayed voussoir and keystone design, side hall plan, mantels and other original woodwork remaining. First house on lot built 1802 is now kitchen wing; main block built 1805; raised from two-and-a-half stories to present height 1881; damaged by fire and repaired 1963. Occupied by James Monroe as secretary of state and in first six months of his presidency; later served as British Legation and as the home of various diplomats and dignataries. 11 sheets (1963, including plot plan, plans, elevations, section, details); 9 ext. photos (1937, 1963), 2 int. photos (1963); 14 data pages (1963). NR, JCL II

Timothy Caldwell House

Cameron House. See Benjamin Ogle Tayloe House (DC-51), 25 Madison Pl., N.W.

Canadian Chancery. See Clarence Moore House (DC-267), 1746 Massachusetts Ave., N.W.

Canal Warehouse (DC-144), N. side of C & O Canal between Warehouse Alley and Wisconsin Ave., entrance at 3222 M St., N.W. (Georgetown). Brick, S. wall built on stone revetment approx. 35′ high, original building approx. 338′ x 75′, two major additions extend to M St., two stories, gable roofs, open plan. Built c. 1838; enlarged twice; originally a tobacco warehouse, later a stable for omnibus line; interior completely altered. 4 ext. photos (1967); 5 data pages (1967).

Capital Garage (DC-279), 1320 New York Ave., N.W. Steel frame, smooth stone facing, ten-bay front, nine-bay flank, ten stories, flat roof, pilaster strips separating bays, ornamental carving consisting of automobile grilles, tires, and bodies, open plan, connecting ramps. Built 1925-26; Arthur Heaton, architect; demolished 1974, sculpture salvaged by Smithsonian Institution. Purported to be largest parking garage in world when built. 4 ext. photos (1974*), 1 int. photo (1974*).

Capital Traction Company Powerhouse (DC-145), 3142 K St., N.W. at foot of Wisconsin Ave. (Georgetown). Brick, approx. L-shaped, 155′-7″ (sixteen bays) x 225′, modified monitor roofs with brick parapets, interior space open from ground floor to roof (approx. six stories), basement beneath. Built 1910-11; demolished 1968. Supplied electrical power for D.C. transportation system from 1911 to 1942. 5 ext. photos (1967), 6 int. photos (1967), 1 photocopy of sketch plan (1967); 18 data pages (1967).

Capital Traction Company Union Station (DC-125), 3600 M St., N.W. (Georgetown). Brick with granite trim, 180′ (front) x 242′, flat roof with parapet, three stories with 140′ central hip-roofed tower, two large arched vehicular doors in end pavilions, rusticated granite facing on first floor. Built 1895-97; Waddy B. Wood, architect; originally designed as terminal for four private transit railway lines with offices, waiting rooms, and car storage areas; steeply sloping site allowed cars to enter at all floor levels; greatly enlarged and altered 1910-11 to accommodate larger double truck cars; M St. facade extended,

Capital Traction Company Union Station

original hipped roofs removed; gradually completely converted to office space. 8 ext. photos (1966), 7 ext. photocopies (c. 1894, c. 1900, c. 1911); 15 data pages (1966).

Carleton, Joseph, House (DC-146), 1052-54 Potomac St., N.W. (Georgetown). Brick, 37'-7" (four-bay front) x 29', two-and-a-half stories with basement exposed in rear, gable roof, shop on first floor, residence above, entrance doors in end bays. Built c. 1800. 2 ext. photos (1967), 1 int. photo (1967), 1 photocopy of sketch plans (1967); 7 data pages (1967). JCL III

Carriage House (DC-250), 1313 31st St., N.W. (Georgetown). Brick, 23'-9" (two-bay front) x 26'-5", one-and-a-half stories, low hipped roof, central pediment on facade, corbeled brick cornice, two large segmental-arched double-leaf doors with brick hoods, loft door above. Built c. 1857; present facade extending building 9' to W. was built in late 19th C. 2 ext. photos (1969); 8 data pages (1969).

Carroll, Daniel, House. See Duddington (DC-8), 2d, E, and F Sts. and New Jersey Ave., S.E.

Cedar Hill. See Frederick Douglass House (DC-97), 1411 W St., S.E.

Central Armature Works. See Commercial Building (DC-308), 629 D St., N.W.

Central National Bank Building (now Apex Liquor Store) (DC-229), 633 Pennsylvania Ave. at C and 7th Sts., N.W. Smooth-faced brownstone ashlar (painted), rock-faced granite string courses and trim, 50-, 40-, and 50-ft. frontages, trapezoidal shape, six and five stories, round corner towers with conical roofs, dormers, south facade of five bays of arched windows in rusticated wall, west facade plain except for arcaded sixth story, north facade six bays of rectangular windows in rusticated wall, first story five pilastered bays (bank facade), cornice of bold projection with consoles and modillions. Built 1888, Alfred Bult Mullet, architect; alterations to first story. 2 ext. photos (1967,1969); 1 data page (1969). JCL III

Chesapeake and Ohio Canal, Georgetown Section (DC-147), running E. and W. parallel to M St., N.W. and one block S. of it (Georgetown). Sandstone and limestone. Georgetown section built c. 1831, Charles B. Fisk and Benjamin Wright, engineers; closed for commercial use 1924; purchased by the National Park Service 1938. Part of a 184.5 mile system linking Georgetown with Cumberland, Md.; one of the greatest engineering undertakings in early 19th C. America. 12 photos (1935, 1967), 3 photocopies (c. 1888, n.d.), photocopy of sketch plan (1967), photocopy of keyed map (1967); 15 data pages (1967). NPS, JCL I

Chinese Community Church (DC-281), 1011 L St., N.W. Brick with limestone trim, two stories with basement, flat roof, projecting entrance pavilion capped by parapet with upswept ends and central cross, lower wing to E. with octagonal window and entrance with tiled pent roof, glazed areas of recessed main entrance and side entrance have mullions arranged in Chinese openwork pattern, interior has 250-seat auditorium, classrooms, pastor's study, stage and kitchen. Built 1956-58; Chatelain, Gauger & Nolan, architects. Nondenominational Protestant church organized in 1935 by Dr. C. C. Hung; purchased residence on present site in 1940. 3 ext. photos (1972*).

Christ Church (Episcopal) (DC-48), 620 G St., S.E. Stuccoed brick, 46'-2" (three-bay front) x 111'-8" (including vestibule, nave, and chancel), one story, gable roof, crenelated bell tower and parapets, projecting entrance vestibule at foot of tower,

Chesapeake and Ohio Canal, Georgetown Section, 1935 view

applied buttresses, Gothic Revival style, cove ceiling over nave, flat ceiling over side aisles. Built 1806-7; traditionally attributed to Benjamin Latrobe, recent attribution to Robert Alexander; extended 20' in 1824; narthex and bell tower added 1849; apse added and stucco applied c. 1877; numerous subsequent alterations, the latest in 1953-54 by architect Horace Peaslee intended to harmonize previous alterations. First place of worship erected by Washington's Episcopal Parish, served Navy Yard area and was attended by several early presidents. 10 sheets (1953, including plot plan, plan, elevations, section, details); 3 ext. photos (1939, 1974*), 1 int. photo (1974*); 2 data pages (1941). NR, JCL II

Christ Church (Episcopal) (DC-243), 3116 O St., N.W. (Georgetown). Pressed red brick with yellow sandstone trim, 60' (three-bay front) x 120' (including former parish hall behind chancel), one story, gable roof with lower cross gable over

Christ Church

parish hall, gabled entrance tower at NE. corner with three-stage
base and arcaded belfry, lancet windows, pointed dormers along
side aisles, Gothic Revival details, exposed scissor truss ceiling,
nave separated from side aisles by sandstone lancet arches
springing from squat columns, stained-glass commemorative windows in chancel, clerestory and aisles, elaborately carved choir
stalls and retable of dark wood. Built 1885-86; Cassell and
Laws, architects; study and Sunday school rooms added 1923;
new chapel built 1967. 3 ext. photos (1968, 1969), 6 int.
photos (1969), photocopy of sketch plan (1968); 21 data pages
(1969). NR, JCL II

Church of the Covenant, during demolition

Church of the Covenant (National Presbyterian Church) (DC-140), SE. corner 18th and N Sts., N.W. at Connecticut Ave. Rusticated stone facing, modified cross plan, cross-gable roof, raised central portion with hipped roof and clerestory windows, tall square arcaded tower at NW. corner, round-arched windows and doors, corner turrets, Romanesque Revival style, interior plaster decoration on arches and spandrels of nave. Built 1887-89; J. C. Cady, architect; tower collapsed during construction, 1888; merged with First Presbyterian Church in 1930; became the National Presbyterian Church in 1947; demolished 1966. 12 ext. photos (1966*, some showing demolition), 2 int. photos (1966).

City Tavern (DC-81), 3206-8 M St., N.W. (Georgetown). Brick, three-and-a-half stories, gable roof with rear dormers. Built 1796; first floor altered for commercial use; remodeled for use as a private club 1961-62; Macomber and Peter, architects. Associated with capital and national history, particularly with Adams and Jefferson. 3 ext. photos (1959), 15 int. photos (1959); 4 data pages (1959). JCL II

Cloud, Abner, House (DC-99), between Canal Rd. and C & O Canal at the intersection of Canal Rd. and Reservoir Rd., N.W. Irregular ashlar, 30' x 28'-8", two-and-a-half stories on sloping site, basement fully exposed on canal side, gable roof, side hall plan. Built c. 1801 by Abner Cloud, a miller. 22 sheets (1964, 1966*, including plot plan, plans, elevations, sections, details); 3 ext. photos (1963); 4 data pages (1964).

Colonial Dames of America, National Headquarters of the National Society of. See Dumbarton House (DC-10), 2715 Q St., N.W. (Georgetown).

Columbia Historical Society. See Christian Heurich Mansion (DC-292), 1307 New Hampshire Ave., N.W.

Columbia Railway Company Car Barns (DC-297), 15th St. and Benning Rd., N.E. Brick, two sections, each one-and-a-half stories, one section has hipped roof with dormers and low central tower, entrance flanked by subsidiary towers, large arched windows; other section has gable roof, corbeled cornice, arched windows flanked by pilaster strips, rear wings, low square towers on corners of both sections. Built by Columbia Railway Company in 1895; building probably served as power-house for short-lived conversion to cable cars 1895-99; converted to bus garage 1942; demolished 1971. The Columbia Line served H St. and connected with the eastern toll gate of the Columbia Turnpike at 15th and H Sts. Originally a horse car line; became last cable railway built in U.S. 1895; converted to electric conduit 1899. 5 ext. photos (1970*), 4 int. photos (1970*).

Commercial Building (Central Armature Works) (DC-308), 629 D St., N.W. Brick with cast-iron shop front, two-bay front, three stories, flat roof, bracketed cornice, arcaded facade, brick hoods with floral drops. Built c. 1870's. 1 ext. photo (1967*).

Commercial Building (Lansburgh's Department Store) (DC-355), SE. corner E and 8th Sts., N.W. Steel frame, white

terra-cotta facing, delicate molded ornament, 120' (seven bays)
x 275' (36 bays), six stories, flat roof. One of several large
department stores built in this area of the city in the early 20th
C. 1 ext. photo (1969*); 1 data page (1969*).

Commercial Building (DC-213), 814 F St., N.W. Brick, 15'-6"
(two-bay front) x 75', flat roof, cast-iron hood molds, cast-iron
and wooden bracketed cornice with central pediment. Built c.
1875; storefront and interior remodeled. 3 ext. photos (1969);
5 data pages (1969). NR, JCL II

Commercial Building (DC-215), 818 F St., N.W. Metal and
brick, 16'-7" front x 75' depth, three stories, flat roof, bracketed
cast-iron cornice. Built c. 1878 with three-bay cast-iron front,
strongly projecting canopies at floor lines; interior and front
almost completely remodeled. 2 ext. photos (1969); 4 data
pages (1969). NR, JCL II

Commercial Building (Old Ebbitt Grill) (DC-315), 1427 F St.,
N.W. Brick, three-bay front, three stories, flat roof, heavy
bracketed cornice, cast-iron hood molds, commercial front.
Probably built 1870s; bar and woodwork from the Ebbitt Hotel
installed on ground floor when hotel demolished in 1926. 1 ext.
photo (1967*). JCL III

Commercial Buildings (DC-333), G St. Between 12th and 13th
  Sts., N.W.

  Building, 204 G St. Brick, six-bay front, four stories, flat
  roof, patterned brick frieze, brownstone sills, bracketed
  cornice, commercial front on first floor, similar facade
  on 12th St. Built late 19th C. 1 ext. photo (1970*).

  Building, NW. corner 12th and G Sts. Brick with smooth
  stone facing on first floor, three bays x nine bays with curving
  corner bay, seven stories, flat roof, strongly projecting
  bracketed cornice, ornamental parapet, flat and arcaded
  window treatment, store front. Built late 19th C.; demolished
  1972. 1 ext. photo (1970*).

  Jordan's Piano Company, 1239 G St. Concrete facing, eight
  stories, flat roof, curving corner with principal windows set in
  curve, only one other small window per floor, storefront. Built
  1950; Johnson and Boutin, architects. 1 ext. photo (1970*).

Commercial Building (David Hayman and Company) (DC-230), 625 Indiana Ave., N.W. Brick, simulating rusticated ashlar on first floor, three-bay front, three stories, cast-iron shop front on first floor, paneled brick pilasters with cast-iron Corinthian capitals, cast-iron hood molds on windows, bracketed cast-iron cornice. Built probably between 1850 and 1860. 1 ext. photo (1969); 1 data page (1969).

Commercial Building (DC-112), 2922 M St., N.W. (George-town). Brick, 32'-6" (two-bay front) x 21'-3", two stories, flat roof, shop front on first floor with bay window, cast-iron balcony across second floor, elaborate corbeled brick cornice, eastern half of a double building. Built probably between 1870 and 1880. 2 ext. photos (1966); 5 data pages (1966).

Commercial Building (DC-222), 809 Market Space (Pennsylvania Ave.), N.W. Brick with cast-iron front, 25' (three-bay front) x 80', four stories, flat roof, paneled pilaster strips, denticulated string courses, Corinthian colonnettes, bracketed cornice with central semicircular pediment. Built 1868 for Thomas L. Hume; first story remodeled. 3 ext. photos (1967, 1969); 4 data pages (1969).

Commercial Building (DC-232), 811 Market Space (Pennsylvania Ave.), N.W. Brick, 25' frontage (three bays), three stories, flat roof, arched windows framed by pilaster strips, brownstone belt courses, brick patternwork and terra-cotta frieze. Built c. 1890; first story remodeled. 1 ext. photo (1969); 1 data page (1969).

Commercial Building (DC-312), 1201 Pennsylvania Ave., N.W. Brick, three stories, gable roof, gabled parapet, round tower at SE. corner above entrance, arcaded fenestration, patterned brickwork, storefront beneath canopy held by metal braces of lion's-head design, rear two-story addition with projecting bays and shop fronts. Probably built c. 1890. 1 ext. photo (1967*).

Commercial Building (Bassin's Restaurant) (DC-313), 1347 Pennsylvania Ave., N.W. Brick with stuccoed facade, approx. 17' (three-bay) front, four stories, flat roof, bracketed modillion cornice with central peak, cast-iron hood molds. Probably built 1870s; first floor altered. 1 ext. photo (1967*).

Commercial Buildings (DC-334), 1922-32 Pennsylvania Ave., N.W. Three 19th C. brick commercial buildings, three stories of

Commercial Building, 1930 Pennsylvania Ave., N.W.

varying heights, each has two shop fronts on lower floor, 1922 has gable roof with dormer and is early 19th C., other two have flat roofs and decorative cornices, built mid 19th C., heavy bracketed cornices with incised design above shop front on 1930 and 1932; all three demolished 1970. 9 ext. photos (1970*), 1 int. photo (1970*).

Commercial Buildings (DC-335), 7th and F Sts., N.W. 19th and early 20th C. commercial buildings, mostly brick, three and four stories, some with cast-iron hood molds, patterened brick, bracketed cornices. 1 general view along N. side of F St. (1970*).

  Union Hardware Building 613 7th St. Brick outlined with light mortar, two-bay front, three stories, flat roof, modillion cornice, projecting bays on second floor. Demolished 1973. 1 ext. photo (1970*).

  Barrister Building, 635 F. St. Brick, stone quoins, nine stories, flat roof with balustrade, Beaux Arts details. Built early 20th C. 1 ext. photo (1970*).

Commercial Building (DC-233), 400 7th St., N.W., N.W. corner 7th and D Sts., N.W. Steel frame, brick veneer, 55' (five bays) x

100' (eight bays), six stories, flat roof, terra-cotta trim, arcaded fenestration, ornamental balconies, modillion cornice. Probably built early 20th C. 1 ext. photo (1969); 1 data page (1969).

Commercial Building (DC-225), 415 7th St., N.W. Brick, stone trim, 25'-7" (three-bay front) x 95', four stories, flat roof, arcaded fenestration, chevron ornament, limestone voussoirs and capitals, polished granite colonnettes, wide frieze of corbeled and patterened brickwork, bracketed cornice. Built c. 1883, perhaps for Elizabeth Cullinan; first story remodeled. 3 ext. photos (1967, 1969); 4 data pages (1969).

Commercial Buildings (DC-309), 308-10 8th St., N.W. Brick, three stories with shop fronts on first floor, 308 has two-bay front, gable roof, brick sawtooth cornice; 310 has three-bay front, flat roof, bracketed modillion cornice, cast-iron hood molds and sills, 308 built early 19th C.; 310 built mid 19th C.; both demolished 1968. 1 ext. photo (1967*).

Commercial Building (DC-234), 616 9th St., N.W. Brick, stone trim, c. 17' front (one bay), three stories, flat roof with false gable, triple fenestration, patterened brick gable. Built c. 1890; lower story remodeled; demolished 1973. 1 ext. photo (1969); 1 data page (1969).

Commercial Building (DC-231), 618 9th St., N.W. Brick, stone, and terra cotta, c. 18' front (two bays), flat roof, arcaded fenestration, molded brick details, false dormer, character perhaps derives from works of R. Norman Shaw. Built c. 1890; lower story remodeled; demolished 1973. 1 ext. photo. (1969); 1 data page (1969).

Convent of the Visitation. See Georgetown Visitation Convent (DC-211), 1500 35th St., N.W. (Georgetown).

Cooke's Row, Villa No. 3 (DC-182), 3013 Q St., N.W. (Georgetown). Brick double house, H-shaped, 48' (six-bay front) x 73' (not including later additions), two-and-a-half stories on raised basement, low-pitched gable roofs with large square central cupola, wide eaves with paired brackets, tall narrow round-arched windows on first floor, rectangular windows with brick hood molds on second floor, three graduated windows in gable ends, paired round-arch entrances in recessed central portion of facade, iron balcony above entrances, side

Corcoran Gallery of Art (later U.S. Court of Claims, now Smithsonian Institution, Renwick Gallery), c. 1880 view

hall plans, Italianate style. Built 1868; Starkweather and Plowman, architects. One of a row of four villas, the end two in the French Second Empire style, the center two, Italianate. Built for Henry D. Cooke, first territorial governor of the District of Columbia. Records deal with eastern half of double house only. 2 ext. photos (1968), 2 int. photos (1968), photocopy of sketch plan (1968); 15 data pages (1968). JCL II

Corcoran Gallery of Art (later U.S. Court of Claims, now Smithsonian Institution, Renwick Gallery) (DC-49), NE. corner Pennsylvania Ave. and 17th St., N.W. Museum. Brick with sandstone trim, 101'-4" (five-bay front) x 126' (eleven bays), two stories on raised basement, mansard roof, projecting entrance pavilion with convex mansard, corner pavilions with slightly lower straight-sided mansards, vermiculated quoins on ground floor, end pavilions have paired Columbian (Indian Corn) pilasters supporting broken entablature and segmental pediment, central pavilion has engaged columns and triangular pediment with medallion of Corcoran in tympanum, eleven second-story windows originally blind niches for monumental statuary, interior features grand central stairway to principal gallery on second floor. Built 1859-60; James Renwick, architect. One of first buildings in the French Second Empire style in the U.S. and also one of first buildings erected as an art gallery. Intended to house private collection of banker and philanthropist W.W. Corcoran; seized by government in 1861 before completion for use as quartermaster's warehouse; reopened as gallery 1874; U.S. Court of Claims building 1899-1964; restored as Renwick Gallery 1967-71 by Universal Restoration, Inc.; Hugh Newell Jacobsen, architect for interior restoration. 3 sheets (1963, including elevations, partial plans); 1 ext. photo (1958), 12 int. photos (1958, 1971*), 10 ext. photocopies (c. 1880*, 1956), 1 photocopy of engraving (n.d.); 23 data pages (1959,1965*, 1971*); 7 photogrammetric stereopairs (1963); HABSI form (1958). NHL, JCL II

Corcoran, Thomas, House (DC-34), 3119-21 M St., N.W. (Georgetown). Brick, three-bay front, three stories, roof either flat or low gable, bracketed modillion cornice, decorative window hoods, shop front on first floor. Thomas Corcoran, leather merchant, mayor of Georgetown and father of W.W. Corcoran, built a house at this location in 1791; facade described above dates from mid 19th C.; demolished 1940. 1 ext. photo (1940, showing demolition).

Corson and Gruman Company. See Ray's Warehouse and Office (DC-148), 3260-62 K Street, N.W. (Georgetown).

Cosmos Club. See Townsend House (DC-273), 2121 Massachusetts Ave., N.W.

Cottage (DC-149), 1222 28th St., N.W. (Georgetown). Frame, flush siding with beaded lower edge, three-bay front, one-and-a-half stories, steeply pitched gable roof with shed dormer, Probably built 1770s. One of oldest structures in Washington, D.C. 2 ext. photos (1937).

Cox, Col. John, House (DC-150), 3339 N St., N.W. (Georgetown). Brick row house, L-shaped, three-bay front, three-and-a-half stories, gable roof, side hall plan, countersunk panels between floors with leaden swags, round-arched entrance with fanlight. This and four adjoining houses built between 1815 and 1818 by Col. Cox who lived in 3339 himself. Cox was mayor of Georgetown 1823-45. 3 ext. photos (1937, 1942). JCL II

Cramphin, Thomas, Building (DC-118), 3209-11 M St., N.W. (Georgetown). Brick double building, each unit is 22' (front) x

60′, three-and-a-half stories, gable roof, first floor shop,
residence above, one large triple window with brick relieving
arch on second floor, small grouped windows on third floor,
this unusual fenestration appears to be original. Built between
1808 and 1813; shop fronts altered. 2 ext. photos (1966); 7
data pages (1966). JCL III

Crandell, Germond, Building (DC-224), 401-07 7th St., N.W.,
NE. corner of 7th and D Sts., N.W. Stucco on brick, stone trim,
75′ (fifteen-bay front) x 54′ (eight bays), four stories, flat roof,
rhythmic arcaded fenestration, molded archivolts, imposts, large
bracketed and modillioned cornice. Built 1877; Germond
Crandell, designer; first story remodeled. 4 ext. photos (1967,
1969); 7 data pages (1969).

Crawford-Cassin House (DC-184), 3017 O St., N.W. (Georgetown). Brick, 37′ (four-bay front) x 72, three stories, gable roof,
two-story wooden porch on east side, NW. portion of rear wing
is three stories, NE. portion is one story, flat-arch stone lintels
with keystones. Built c. 1816; interiors reveal mid 19th C.
alteration; house further altered for use as girls' school in early
20th C. Example of free-standing Federal house with some
gardens remaining. Home of Comdr. Stephen Cassin, naval hero
in War of 1812. 2 ext. photos (1968), 3 int. photos (1968),
photocopy of sketch plan (1968); 13 data pages (1968, 1969).

Culver, Frederick B., House (DC-220), 809 E. St., N.W. Brick,
26′-4″ (three-bay front) x 100′, four-and-a-half stories above
basement, gable roof, three-story back building with shed roof,
string courses, window cornices, wooden modillion cornice,
dormers, side hall plan. Built c. 1868, Zephaniah Jones, builder;
grade level lowered c. 1871; basement remodeled into store;
demolished 1973. 2 ext. photos (1969), 2 int. photos (1969); 5
data pages (1969).

Cutts, Richard, House (Dolley Madison House) (DC-58), SE.
corner H St. and Madison Pl., N.W. Stuccoed brick, three-bay
front, three-and-a-half stories on raised basement, low hipped
roof, narrow frieze openings with louvers, cast-iron gallery
across first floor, entrance in rear addition. Built c. 1818-20 by
Richard Cutts, brother-in-law of Dolley Madison; originally a
two-and-a-half story house with gable roof and side hall plan;
extensively altered; renovated 1967-68 as part of Lafayette
Square redevelopment. Home of the widowed Dolley Madison

1837-49 and a center of Washington social life; Gen. McClellan's headquarters during Civil War; purchased by Cosmos Club 1886. 1 ext. photo (1958); 1 data page (1958); HABSI form (1957). JCL II

Czechoslovakian Embassy (former). See Christian Hauge House (DC-262), 2349 Massachusetts Ave., N.W. at intersection of 24th St.

Daly, Carroll, House (DC-205), 1306 35th St., N.W. (Georgetown). Brick row house, L-shaped, 16′ (three-bay front) x 30′, ell is 12′ x 16′, two stories on raised basement, flat roof, pressed brick facade with molded brick trim above doors and windows, corbeled cornice. Probably built between 1883 and 1886; interior extensively altered. 1 ext. photo (1968*); 21 data pages (1968*).

Daughters of the American Revolution, National Society of. See Memorial Continental Hall (DC-282), 1776 D St., N.W.

John Davidson House

Davidson, John, House (DC-102), 1220 Wisconsin Ave., N.W. (Georgetown). Brick, 23′ (three-bay front) x approx. 100′ (including shed-roofed rear ells), four stories, gable roof, modified side hall plan, first floor shop. Built c. 1790; one of few substantially unaltered 18th C. buildings in Georgetown commercial district; demolished 1972. 2 ext. photos (1966); 5 data pages (1966).

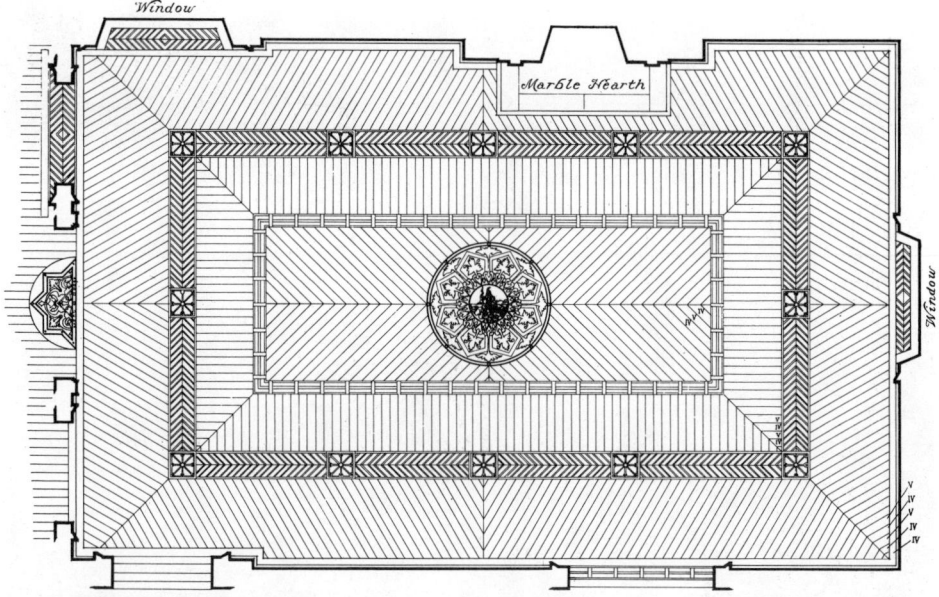

Decatur House, parquetry floor

Davidson, Samuel, House. See Evermay (DC-61), 1623 28th St., N.W. (Georgetown).

Decatur-Gunther House. See John S. Williams House (DC-29), 2812 N St., N.W. (Georgetown).

Decatur House (National Trust for Historic Preservation) (DC-16), 748 Jackson Pl., N.W. Historic house museum and offices of the National Trust. Brick with stone trim, 51′ (three-bay front) x 45′, three stories, low hipped roof, long two-story service wing and stable at rear, severe facade, flat stone lintels with bull's-eye corner blocks, entrance has elliptical fanlight and side lights, central hall plan, notable three-part entrance vestibule with vaulted ceilings and recessed alcoves. Built 1818-19; Benjamin H. Latrobe, architect. First residence on Lafayette Square; built for Com. Stephen Decatur, hero of War of 1812 and subduer of Tripoli pirates; residence of notable statesmen and diplomats including Henry Clay and Martin Van Buren; purchased in 1871 by Edward Beale, who added brownstone trim to first floor windows and installed parquetry floors of rare woods in second floor public rooms; exterior alterations removed 1944; Thomas T. Watermann, restoration

Devore-Chase House

architect; service wing altered for office use 1960; attic converted to office space 1972. 23 sheets (1937, including plans, elevations, details); 10 ext. photos (1937 showing late 19th C. alterations, 1964*), 33 int. photos (1937, 1964*, 1972* including 12 views of attic before alteration); 2 data pages (1937). NHL, JCL I

De La Roche-Jewell Tenant House (DC-179), 1320 30th St., N.W. (Georgetown). Frame row house, 19' (three-bay front) x 40', two stories, gable roof, bracketed wooden modillion cornice, cast-iron ornamental lintels, two-column flat-roofed entrance porch with modillion cornice. Built c. 1865; interior altered in 20th C. Typical mid-19th C. rental housing; one of three identical houses. 1 ext. photo (1968), photocopy of sketch plan (1968); 9 data pages (1968).

Devore-Chase House (DC-288), 2000 24th St., N.W., NE. corner of 24th St. & Wyoming Ave. Limestone ashlar, 88'-6" (nine-bay front with forecourt between two-bay end pavilions) x 60'-3", two stories, hipped roofs, pedimented entrance pavilion, corner

quoins, modillion cornice, modified central hall plan, French
18th-century details. Built 1931; William Lawrence Bottomley
(1884-1951), architect. Noteworthy for fine proportions, details, and interiors. 4 ext. photos (1972), 5 int. photos (1972);
10 data pages (1972).

District Building (DC-314), SE. corner of 14th and E Sts., N.W.
Marble on granite base, 190′ (nine-bay front) x 241′ (thirteen
bays), U-shaped above first floor, five stories with exposed
basement and subbasement, entrance and end pavilions project
slightly, basement and first floor serve as rusticated base for
monumental Corinthian pilasters which separate bays on second
through fourth floors, windows on fifth floor flanked by heroic
allegorical figures and decorative cartouches; interior marble
stair opposite main entrance, principal offices of paneled wood
and large meeting room on fifth floor, Beaux Arts style. Built
1904-8; Cope and Stewardson, architects; De Nesti, sculptor;
interior alterations. Has housed the municipal government of
the District of Columbia, in its various forms, since its erection.
1 ext. photo (1970*). NR, JCL II

District of Columbia City Hall (DC-41), 451 Indiana Ave., N.W.,
S. side of Judiciary Square. Indiana limestone, 240′ x 176′,
E-shaped with wings projecting farther than central pavilion,
two stories on exposed basement, low hipped roof, central
pedimented Ionic hexastyle portico, wings have monumental
distyle *in-antis* elevations, Greek Revival style. Central section begun 1820, E. wing completed 1826, W. wing completed 1849;
George Hadfield, architect; addition across entire N. side, 1881;
virtually reconstructed in 1916 when exterior changed from
stuccoed brick to limestone, about 25% of original material
retained; interior completely redesigned. Originally a city hall,
soon became a U.S. courthouse, now houses D.C. Superior
Court; to be restored as office of the mayor. 5 ext. photos
(1935, 1971*), 4 int. photos (1971*). NHL, JCL I

District of Columbia Engine Company No. 1 Firehouse
(DC-86), 1643 K St., N.W. Brick, two-bay front, two stories,
flat roof with balustraded wooden platform, modillion cornice
with dentils and end brackets, two vehicular doors, double
windows above. Built 1867; in use until 1960; demolished.
Company organized in 1836 as Union Volunteer Fire Company.
Became Engine Company No. 1 in 1864 when part-paid city fire
department was first organized. Moved to 1643 K St. in 1867. 1
ext. photo (prior to 1960).

District of Columbia Engine Company No. 2 Firehouse (DC-350), 719 12th St., N.W. Brick, three-bay front, two stories, tile hipped roof with wide eaves over front portion, lower flat roof over rear of building, three equipment doors with heavy quoins, second floor windows have quoins and pediments, patterned frieze of bricks and stucco. Built 1910. 1 ext. photo (1970*), 1 int. photo (1970*).

District of Columbia Engine Company No. 4 Firehouse (DC-87), 931 R St., N.W. Brick with stone trim, two-bay front,

District of Columbia Engine Company No. 2 Firehouse

two stories, flat roof, elaborate parapet with central pediment,
corbeled cornice, two vehicular doors, arched windows above.
Built c. 1885; new front built in 1960s. Building originally built
for Engine Company No. 7; occupied by Engine Company No.
4, the city's first all-black company, in 1940. 1 ext. photo
(prior to 1960).

District of Columbia Engine Company No. 5 Firehouse. See
Bank of Columbia (DC-119), 3210 M St., N.W. (Georgetown).

District of Columbia Engine Company No. 6 Firehouse (DC-
88), 438 Massachusetts Ave., N.W. Brick, two-bay front, two
stories, flat roof, corbeled cornice, two vehicular doors, two
arched windows above. Originally built for the volunteer
Metropolitan Hook & Ladder Company in 1855; became
firehouse for Engine Company No. 6 in 1879; remodeled in
1960 (including overhead doors). 1 ext. photo (prior to 1960).

District of Columbia Engine Company No. 9 Firehouse
(DC-89), 1624 U St., N.W. Brick with ashlar facing on first
floor, two-and-a-half stories, flat roof, low central hipped-roof
tower flanked by parapets, curving second-story bay supported
on carved lion mask. Built 1893; engine company moved across
U St. in 1966. 1 ext. photo (prior to 1960).

District of Columbia Engine Company No. 10 Firehouse
(DC-90), 1341 Maryland Ave., N.E. Brick with stone trim,
two-bay front, two stories, flat roof, central pediment over
corbeled cornice, bands of stone and brick on first floor, belt
course with cornice, pilaster strips with stone caps, date plaque.
Built 1894. 1 ext. photo (prior to 1960).

District of Columbia Engine Company No. 12 Firehouse
(DC-91), 1626 North Capitol St. at Quincy Pl. Brick with stone
trim, two-and-a-half stories, cross-gable roof, stepped and
shaped gables with Palladian windows, two vehicular doors.
Built 1897. 1 ext. photo (prior to 1960).

District of Columbia Engine Company No. 15 Firehouse
(DC-92), 1345 V St., S.E. (formerly 2100 14th St., S.E.). Brick
channeled to simulate rusticated ashlar on lower facade, two
stories, hipped roof, three-story side tower, two equipment
doors, balcony with recessed loggia above. Built 1897; demolished 1967; new firehouse erected on site. 1 ext. photo (prior to
1960).

District of Columbia Engine Company No. 17 Firehouse (DC-93), 1227 Monroe St., N.E. Brick, three-bay front, two stories, flat roof, four-story corner tower with overhanging hipped roof, one vehicular door, arched windows above. Built 1902 for Chemical Engine Company No. 4; reorganized as Engine Company No. 17 in 1905. 2 ext. photos (prior to 1960, 1961).

District of Columbia Engine Company No. 21 Firehouse (DC-94), 1763 Lanier Pl., N.W. Stuccoed brick, two-and-a-half stories, tile gable roof, shaped front gable, tall chimneys joined by arch, two vehicular doors, grouped windows, Spanish Mission style. Built 1908. 1 ext. photo (prior to 1960).

District of Columbia Engine Company No. 22 Firehouse (DC-95), 5760 Georgia Ave., N.W. Brick with stone trim, three-bay front, two-and-a-half stories, flat roof, modillion cornice, pilaster strips, three vehicular doors, double windows above. Built 1897 for Chemical Engine Company No. 2; reorganized as Engine Company No. 22 in 1908; third bay a later addition. 1 ext. photo (prior to 1960).

District of Columbia Truck Company No. 4 Firehouse (DC-96), 219 M St., N.W. Brick with rusticated ashlar veneer on first story front, two-and-a-half stories with pedimented central aedicula, arched fire doors with keystones carved with hook and ladder design. Built 1896, remodeled 1960s (ashlar veneer and arched doors replaced with brick veneer and rectangular doors). The same truck company (originally called Truck Company D) has occupied the building since its construction. 2 ext. photos (prior to 1960).

Dodge, Francis, Warehouse (DC-100). 1006 Wisconsin Ave., N.W., now joined to the adjacent building and both are numbered 1000 Wisconsin Ave. (Georgetown). Brick, 25'-10" (three-bay front) x 47'-6", two-and-a-half stories, gable roof, projecting pulley housing on dormer, open plan, S. wall of rubble masonry probably part of stone house previously on site. Built late 18th C.; one of a group of three warehouses remaining from Georgetown's maritime era. 1 ext. photo (1966), 3 int. photos (1966); 9 data pages (1966). JCL II

Dodge, Robert P., House (DC-246), 1534 28th St., N.W. (Georgetown). Stuccoed brick, originally L-shaped, 60' (four-

bay front) x 54', two stories with basement fully exposed in
rear, gable roof, hipped roof tower in reentrant angle, Italianate
style. Built 1850-53; Andrew Jackson Downing and Calvert
Vaux, architects. One of two similar "Suburban Villas"
designed by the architects for brothers Robert and Francis
Dodge. Extensively remodeled c. 1936 when hood molds,
canopies, cornice brackets, and front porch removed; house
raised to four stories in rear, two-story portico added to front,
interior completely remodeled in Georgian style. 2 ext. photos
(1968, 1969), 2 int. photos (1969), 3 photocopies of original
plans and plates (1857), 2 copies of old ext. photos (1900,
1933); 16 data pages (1969). JCL III

Double House (DC-152), 1061-63 Potomac St., N.W. (Georgetown). Brick, four-bay front, three-and-a-half stories, gabled
roof, flat-arched brick lintels with keystones, belt courses
beneath second and third floor windows at sill level. Built early
19th C. 1 ext. photo (1937).

Double House and Stable (DC-56), 304-6 11th St., S.W. Brick,
each unit three-bay front, three stories on raised basement, low
roof, probably flat, widely projecting cornice with brackets and
modillions, one-story semicircular bay, decorative hood on
incised consoles over entrance, window lintels have antefixae, side
hall plans; two-story brick stable at rear. Built probably 1870's;
demolished. 2 ext. photos (1958, one of stable).

Douglass, Frederick, House (John Van Hook House, Cedar Hill)
(DC-97), 1411 W St., S.E. Historic house museum of the National
Park Service. Brick, L-shaped, 42'-8" (five-bay front) x 70'-6"
(including rear frame wing), two-and-a-half stories, gable roof,
central hall plan, bracketed cornice, one-story wooden porch
with Doric columns and trellising across front, three-sided oriel
in center of second story under cross gable, two one-story brick
bays off east parlor. Built c. 1855 by Union Land Association;
purchased 1877 by Frederick Douglass, runaway slave, aboli-
tionist, editor, and statesman. Douglass added parlor bays,
frame kitchen wing and numerous outbuildings (now demolished). Preserved as a memorial to Douglass after his death in
1895; restored by National Park Service, 1971-72. 8 sheets
(1964, including plot plan, plans, elevations, section, details); 7
ext. photos (1963), 2 int. photos showing restoration (1971*),
2 ext. photocopies (c. 1894-1900, c. 1897); 6 data pages
(1964). NPS, JCL II

Frederick Douglass House

Doxiadis Associates. See Potomac Lodge No. 5 (DC-153), 1058 Thomas Jefferson St., N.W. (Georgetown).

Duddington (Daniel Carroll House) (DC-8), 2d, E, and F Sts. and New Jersey Ave., S.E. Brick, approx. 70′ (nine-bay front) x 35′, two-and-a-half stories on raised basement, gable roof, three-bay projecting central pavilion with pediment, one-story four-columned wooden entrance porch, most windows flat-arched with keystone lintels, central hall plan. Built 1793-94 by Daniel Carroll; demolished 1886; mantels and stairway transferred to 820 17th St., N.W., also now demolished. One of first great mansions of Washington; Maj. L'Enfant ordered partially completed house demolished because original site lay within the line of New Jersey Ave.; rebuilt on present site at government expense. 2 sheets (1936, details of stairway); 6 photos of mantels and stairway (1935, 1937), 2 ext. photocopies (1884, n.d.); 3 data pages (c. 1936).

Dumbarton House (Bellevue, Rittenhouse Place, now National Headquarters of the National Society of Colonial Dames of

America) (DC-10), originally located at the end of what is now Q St. above Rock Creek, since 1915 at 2715 Q St., N.W. (Georgetown). Historic house museum. Brick, five-part mansion plan with wings and connecting hyphens, two-and-a-half stories, gable roofs on wings, hipped roof on main block, central block has five bays with slightly projecting entrance bay, cross gable, one-story wooden entrance portico with heavy paired Ionic columns and wide entablature, two-story circular bows on rear, Doric cornice, central hall plan. Probably built 1799 for Samuel Jackson on part of very early land grant called "Rock of Dumbarton"; remodeling in early 19th C. attributed to Benjamin Latrobe, at that time second-story windows lengthened, balconies, portico, and rear bays added. Main block moved to present location in 1915 when Q St. extended across Rock Creek Park; became national headquarters of Colonial Dames in 1928; restored 1931, Horace Peaslee, restoration architect. 3 ext. photos (1942, 1974*). JCL II

Duncanson-Cranch House (Barney Neighborhood House) (DC-128), 468-70 N St., S.W. Brick double house designed to appear as a single unit, stone trim, 44' facade (six-bays), three stories on raised basement, gable roof, second-story windows set in stuccoed blind arches, splayed stone lintels, paired modillion cornice, belt course below second floor, entrances on side, W. side entrance has semicircular fanlight and is flanked by semicircular-arched windows in sunken arches. Built c. 1794-95; attributed to William Lovering, architect for the Greenleaf Syndicate; rehabilitated 1964-66 as part of Harbour Square urban renewal development. From 1904 to 1960 was headquarters for Barney Neighborhood House. 4 ext. photos (1937, 1974*), NR, JCL II

Duncanson, William, House. See The Maples (DC-5), 630 South Carolina Ave., S.E.

Duvall Foundry (DC-154), 1050 30th St., N.W., S. side of C & O Canal (Georgetown). Brick, 26' (three-bay front) x 88'-5" (ten bays), two-and-a-half stories with basement, low gabled roof, pilaster strips, corbeled brick cornice. Typical mid 19th C. commercial building. Built c. 1856; interior completely altered; foundations rebuilt 1974; to be renovated for shops and offices as part of Georgetown Harbor Project. 3 ext. photos (1967), 1 ext. photocopy (c. 1914); 12 data pages (1967). JCL III

Duvall Foundry, c. 1914 view

Eagle House. See John Mountz House (DC-18), 3016 M St., N.W. (Georgetown).

Easby House (DC-7), 2600 Block of D St., N.W. Brick, 50′-8″ (seven-bay facade including two-bay addition to E.) x 28′, two-and-a-half stories (eastern addition slightly higher), gable roof, sawtooth brick cornice. Built c. 1830; extensively altered by addition of two vehicular doors; demolished. 2 sheets (1936, including plans, elevations, details); 4 ext. photos (1936).

Eastern Market (DC-291), 7th St., S.E., between C St. and North Carolina Ave. Red brick, originally approx. 50′ (five bays) x 180′ (twenty bays), later extended to 300′ (thirty-two bays), open one-story plan with two-story connection between original building and addition, slate hipped roof, iron trussing exposed on interior, principal entrance in three-bay projection centered on long facade, on original section windows alternate with doors in narrow bays, both are round-headed with keystone and voussoir motif, corbeled brick trim, unattached open shed for farmers runs length of 7th St. facade. Built 1872-73; Adolf Cluss, architect; addition to N. 1908. Last of city's markets to continue operation. 9 ext. photos (1971*), 3 int. photos (1971*). NR, JCL II

Eastern Market

Embassy of the Arab Republic of Egypt. See Joseph Beale House (DC-257), 2301 Massachusetts Ave., N.W. at intersection of Massachusetts Ave., R St., and Sheridan Circle, N.W.

Embassy of the Federal Republic of Cameroon Chancery. See Christian Hauge House (DC-262), 2349 Massachusetts Ave., N.W. at intersection of 24th St.

Embassy of Luxembourg. See Alexander Stewart House (DC-272), 2200 Massachusetts Ave., N.W.

Episcopal Church Home. See Bowie-Sevier House (DC-60), 3124 Q St., N.W. (Georgetown).

Estes Mill Ruins (DC-40), Rock Creek Park, N. of present Calvert St. Bridge, N.W. Former Rock Creek valley water mill, ruinous. 1 copy of old photo (n.d.) (In background of photograph is steel viaduct of Rock Creek Railway at Calvert St. Built c. 1892).

Evening Star Building (DC-316), NW. corner 11th St. and Pennsylvania Ave., N.W. Steel frame with rusticated and smooth-faced marble veneer, L-shaped, 51' (three-bay facade) x 236' (including addition), ten stories, flat roof with balustrade, elaborately detailed in Classical Beaux Arts style. Built 1898; Marsh and Peter, architects; major addition to rear 1918. Home of the *Evening Star* from 1898 to 1955. 1 ext. photo (1967*). JCL III

Everett, Edward H., House (Turkish Embassy) (DC-258), 1606 23d St., N.W. at Sheridan Circle. Brick with limestone facing, irregular plan, basically rectangular block with wing to S., 91'-6" (main facade) x 66'-3", three stories with two-story ballroom wing, low hipped roof behind balustrade, rusticated ground floor, two-story semicircular portico with fluted composite columns, semicircular-arched second floor windows with balustraded balconies on consoles, roof garden with wooden trellis roof above ballroom wing, neoclassical Beaux Arts style, central grand stair, marble mantels, elaborate plasterwork and woodwork, cast-iron grilles, stained glass. Built 1910-15 for multimillionaire industrialist Edward H. Everett; George Oakley Totten, architect. Occupied by Turkish Embassy since 1932. 1 ext. photo (1970*), 8 int. photos (1970*), photocopy of plan (1972*); 21 data pages (1970-73*).

Evermay (Samuel Davidson House) (DC-61), 1623 28th St., N.W. (Georgetown). Brick, main block has five-bay front, two-and-a-half stories, gable roof, central hall plan. Built 1801 for Samuel Davidson; Nicholas King, designer; Nicholas Hedges, carpenter / builder; interior alterations through 1811; house Victorianized in 1877; renovated and enlarged 1923 and following; now a five-part plan with hyphens and wings, interior largely altered. 2 ext. photos (1942). NHL, JCL II

Eynon Building (Regency Row) (DC-124), 3407 M St., N.W.
(Georgetown). Brick, 29'-7" (front) x approx. 50', two stories,
flat roof, projecting second story oriel with stamped metal
facing, shop on first floor, apartment above, part of a row of
ten two-story and three-story buildings extending 180' along M
St. Built c. 1909. 3 ext. photos (1966); 6 data pages (1966).

F Street Club. See Alexander Ray House (DC-44), 1925 F St.,
N.W.

Fahnestock, Gibson, House (Republic of China Chancery)
(DC-259), 2311 Massachusetts Ave., N.W. Brick with limestone
facing on principal facade, 42' (three-bay front) x 92'-6",
three-and-a-half stories, full story and an additional attic story
under slate mansard roof, rusticated first floor, two-story fluted
Corinthian pilasters flank second and third story windows,
decorative grilles on second floor windows, segmental pediments on dormers, 18th C. French decorative details. Built
1909-10; Nathan C. Wyeth, architect. 2 ext. photos (1970*), 2
int. photos (1970*), photocopy of floor plans (1972*); 13 data
pages (1970-73*).

Fairbanks, Henry Parker, House. See Woodrow Wilson House
(DC-133), 2340 S St., N.W.

Female Union Benevolent Society. See John Lutz House
(DC-105), 1255 Wisconsin Ave., N.W. (Georgetown).

Fenwick, Teresa, House (Thomas Parrott House) (DC-83), 3512
P St., N.W. (Georgetown). Brick, 23'-10" (three-bay front) x
34'-9", two-and-a-half stories with basement exposed in rear,
gable roof, end chimneys, side hall plan. Built 1826; restored
1950s. 10 sheets (1963, including plot plan, plans, elevations,
details); 6 ext. photos (1963, 1969), 3 int. photos (1963); 21
data pages (1963, 1969).

Findley House (DC-192), 3606 N St., N.W. (Georgetown).
Frame row house, approx. 17' (three-bay front) x 35', two
stories, gable roof. Built 1866 as rental property. 1 ext. photo
(1968*); 16 data pages (1968*).

Firehouses. See District of Columbia Fire Companies.

Firemen's Insurance Company Building (DC-235), 303 7th St.,
at Indiana Ave., N.W. Brick, 35' x 60', five stories with

octagonal corner tower and mansard roof, asymmetrical facades, small-scale ornament. Probably built shortly before 1887; ground story and interior modernized; original gold dome on corner tower removed. 1 ext. photo (1969), 1 ext. photocopy (n.d.); 1 data page (1969).

First Baptist Church of Georgetown (DC-241), SE. corner 27th St. and Dumbarton Ave., N.W. (Georgetown). Brick, basically rectangular with slightly projecting transepts, one story with raised basement, gable roof, two low hipped-roof towers at NE. and NW. corners, stained-glass lancet windows, Gothic Revival details; sanctuary above Sunday school and meeting rooms, pressed tin ceiling in sanctuary. Built 1882; interior remodeled 1904 and 1940. Church founded 1862 by Sandy Alexander, Baptist minister and freed slave. First congregation of the Baptist denomination in Georgetown. 1 ext. photo (1968), photocopy of sketch plan (1968); 13 data pages (1969).

Fitzhugh, Emma S., House (Philippine Embassy) (DC-260), 2253 R St., N.W. Stone facing, rusticated on ground floor 58'-3" (three-bay facade) x 64'-1", three stories, widely overhanging eaves with scroll brackets, second floor windows have triangular pediments on scroll consoles, third floor windows have small iron grilles, Mediterranean details. Built 1904; Wood, Donn, and Deming, architects. Example of smaller residence in the Massachusetts Ave. Embassy Row area. 1 ext. photo (1970*), 4 int. photos (1970*); 2 data pages (1970-73*).

Florida House, Headquarters of Florida State Society. See Edwin C. Manning House (DC-330), 200 East Capitol St.

Ford's Theater (DC-82), 511 10th St., N.W. Museum. Brick with stone trim, 71' (five-bay front) x 108', three stories, gable roof, arcaded first story with five entrance doors, pilaster strips carry wide entablature, denticulated cornice, gable end forms pediment, two curving interior balconies supported by cast-iron columns, principal boxes framed by composite pilasters, ornamental plasterwork. Built 1863; James J. Gifford, architect. Scene of the assassination of Abraham Lincoln by John Wilkes Booth in April 1865; theater closed and converted to government office building; front wall collapsed killing 22 employees in 1893; used as a storehouse and then a museum; restored to its 1865 appearance 1964-68 by the National Park Service; reopened as a theater with museum in the basement. 17 sheets

Ford's Theater, restored interior

(1962*, including plot plan, plans, elevations, sections, details); 1 ext. photo (1968*), 3 int. photos (1968*). NPS, JCL II

Forrest-Marbury House (DC-68), 3350 M St., N.W. (Georgetown). Brick with stone trim, 35' (three-bay front) x 55', three stories, flat roof, splayed lintels with keystones. Built between 1788 and 1790 by Gen. Uriah Forrest; originally two-and-a-half stories with gable roof, free standing mansion; two-story addition to E. built between 1836 and 1860; third story added before 1860; first floor converted to shops, upper floors to apartments; present cornice reproduced from fragments of original, added 1950s. Scene of discussions effecting the establishment of the federal city. Later home of John Marbury, a principal in the case *Marbury* vs. *Madison*. 5 ext. photos (1959), 2 int. photos (1959), 1 ext. photocopy (c. 1860); 2 data pages (1959); HABSI form (1959). NR, JCL I

Foxhall-McKenney House (DC-66), 3123 Dumbarton Ave., N.W. (Georgetown). Brick, five-bay front, two-and-a-half stories

Franklin School

on raised basement, gable roof, central hall plan, one-story
pedimented wooden portico on S. facade. Built c. 1813 by
Henry Foxhall as a wedding gift for his daughter Mrs. Samuel
McKenney. 2 ext. photos (1942). JCL II

Franklin School (Public)(DC-289), SE. corner 13th and K Sts.,
N.W. Brick with stone trim, 147'-6" (nine-bay front) x 79'-9"
(six bays), three stories plus partially exposed basement, facade
has central 78' high section with mansard roof and two flanking
wings 66' high with flat roofs, octagonal ventilating towers at
four corners and flanking central pavilion, cast-iron window
hoods, corbeled cornice, ornamental banding of white stone,
two entrances and symmetrical interior reflect original segrega-
tion by sex, large hall with clerestory lighting on third floor.
Built 1865-69; Adolf Cluss, architect. Innovative school design
which won prizes at international exhibitions; attended by
children of several presidents; site of first wireless telephone
message transmitted by Alexander Graham Bell. 9 ext. photos
(1969*), 13 int. photos (1969*). NR, JCL II

Fraser, George, House (Scott-Thropp House, later Golden
Parrot Restaurant) (DC-318), NE. corner R and 20th Sts., N.W.
at Connecticut Ave. Brick with stone trim, facade has three
irregular bays, three stories on high rusticated basement, hipped
roof, smooth stone belt courses and quoins, modillion cornice,
colonnaded entrance porch with balustraded deck, high brick
garden wall to E. and N., low stone wall to S. and W. Built
1890 for New York merchant George Fraser; Hornblower and
Marshall, architects; purchased 1901 by Miriam Scott Thropp;
lower floor became tea room in 1932; converted to restaurant
1950. 1 ext. photo (1968*).

French, Robert, House. See Oak Hill (DC-42), Connecticut
Ave., near Cathedral Ave., N.W.

Friendship House. See The Maples (DC-5), 630 South Carolina
Ave., S.E.

Gallaudet College (DC-300), 7th St. and Florida Ave., N.E.
Founded in 1864 as nation's first and only institution of higher
learning for the deaf, landscape design by Frederick Law
Olmsted and Calvert Vaux in 1866; nine buildings designed by
Frederick C. Withers between 1865 and 1880s include Chapel
Hall, College Hall, President's House, professors' houses, and

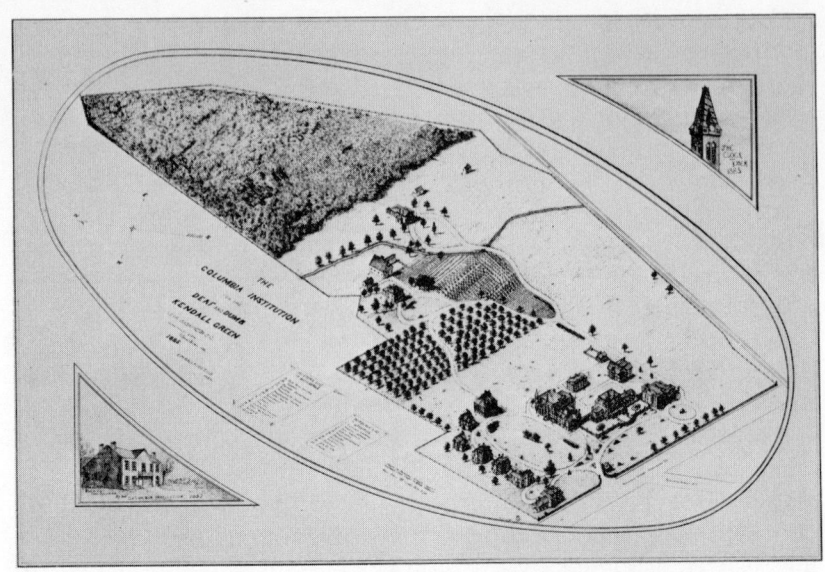

Gallaudet College, original plan for grounds

gymnasium with indoor swimming pool; an attempt to integrate architecture and natural surroundings. Founded by Amos Kendall; first president was Edward Miner Gallaudet. 3 ext. photos of professors' houses and gatehouse (1970*), 11 photocopies of original drawings of grounds, swimming bath/ gymnasium, and professor's house (1874*, 1880*, 1885*). NR, JCL I

Chapel Hall (DC-301), 7th St. and Florida Ave., N.E. Brownstone with bands of lighter colored Ohio stone, 187'-6" x approx. 65', three sections of varying heights, basically one story, tall central section contains chapel / auditorium, W. wing was college dining room, E. wing was lecture hall and primary dining room with a half story of dormitory rooms, hipped roofs with flat decks, patterned slate covering, square clock tower at SW. corner of central section, arched windows of chapel and arches of entrance porch have contrasting stone voussoir, wooden spire on chapel roof. One of earliest examples of Ruskinian Gothic collegiate architecture in U.S. Built 1867-70; Frederick C. Withers, architect. 3 ext. photos (1970*), 2 int. photos (1970*), 6 photocopies of original drawings (1868*). NHL, JCL II

College Hall (DC-302), 7th St. and Florida Ave., N.E. Brick 49
with brownstone banding and window trim, modified hipped
roof, southern section is three stories, northern section is
three-and-a-half stories, full basement, gabled wall dormers of
various sizes, designs in black brick on dormers and in frieze
between first floor window heads, round tower on corbeled
base at NW. corner, joined to Chapel Hall by covered arcade
at SE. corner, Ruskinian Gothic style, built as dormitory and
administration building with second floor museum and
library. Built 1875-78; Frederick C. Withers, architect. 4 ext.
photos (1970*), 8 photocopies of original drawings (1875-
76*).

President's House (DC-303), 7th St. and Florida Ave.,N.E.,
W. of entrance gate. Brick with brownstone trim, 95'-8"
(including service wing) x 58', two-and-a-half stories with
two-story wing to W., hipped roof with flat deck, projecting
entrance pavilion with decorative gable,brownstone entrance
surround, relieving arches above first floor windows,
gable-roofed and jerkinhead dormers, one-story frame veranda
along E. side, modified central hall plan, period interiors are
well preserved. Built 1867-68; Frederick C. Withers, architect;
frame stair wing at NW. corner probably added 1887. 2 ext.
photos (1970*), 6 int. photos (1970*), 8 photocopies of
original drawings (1867*). NR, JCL II

Gallaudet College, Chapel Hall, architect's original drawing

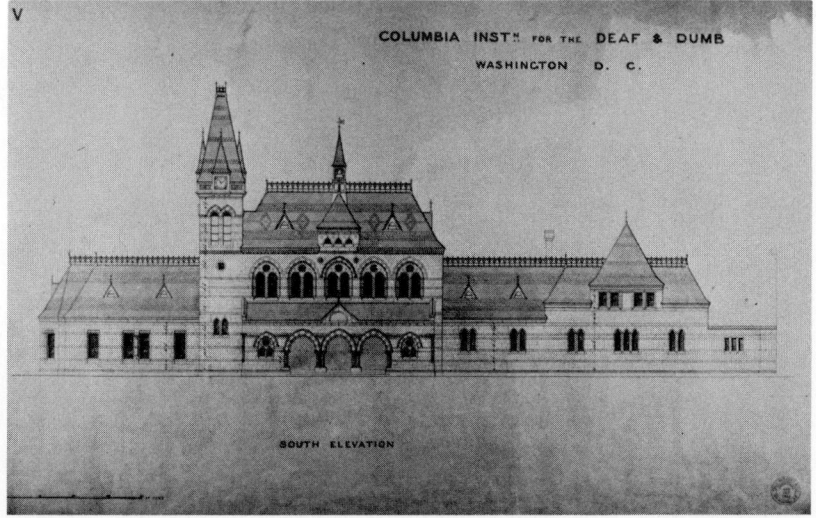

Georgetown Street Furniture

Gannt-Williams House. See Isaac Owens House (DC-62), 2806 N
St., N.W. (Georgetown).

Gazebo (DC-155), rear of 3233 N St., N.W. (Georgetown). Wooden, one story, gable roof with pediment ends, corner pilasters, octagonal cupola, Greek Revival style. Built c. 1840; restored. 1 ext. photo (1937). JCL III

Georgetown Club, The. See House (DC-109), 1530 Wisconsin Ave., N.W. (Georgetown).

Georgetown Market (DC-123), 3276 M St., N.W. (Georgetown). Brick, 40′ (three-bay front) x 200′ (eleven bays), one story, low gable roof, open plan, doors and windows have round-arch openings, bracketed cornice, central parapet. Built 1866 on foundations of a 1796 market. 3 ext. photos (1966); 7 data pages (1966). NR, JCL II

Georgetown Street Furniture (DC-252), various locations within the limits of the old city of Georgetown. Study of elements of the streetscape remaining from the 19th and early 20th centuries. Includes street lamps, call boxes, traffic lights, paving patterns, street car tracks, and coal chutes. 14 ext. photos (1969); 7 data pages (1969).

Georgetown Town Hall. See Bank of Columbia (DC-119), 3210 M St., N.W. (Georgetown).

Georgetown University

Healy Building (DC-248), Campus of Georgetown University, 250′ W. of main entrance gates at 37th and O Sts., N.W. (Georgetown). Hammer-faced Potomac gneiss ashlar on three elevations, brick on W. elevation, roughly rectangular with projecting pavilion blocks at N. and S., older buildings adjoin rear to form U-shaped courtyard, 310′ (twenty-nine-bay front) x 74′ (at S. end), four-and-a-half stories with raised basement, gable roof on central portion, steep hipped roofs on N. and S. pavilions, 200′-tall central clock spire, secondary spire above stair tower at SW. corner, square towers for fire stairs at corners of pavilions, main entrance with stone porch in N. pavilion; elaborate interiors feature paneled ceilings, wainscotting, and painted ceiling and wall trim; major interior spaces are Gaston Hall with paneled hammer beam ceiling and

Georgetown University, Healy Building

elaborately painted walls and Riggs Library stack area with four levels of cast-iron stacks. Built 1877-79, interiors not finished until 1909; Smithmeyer and Pelz, architects. Strikingly sited on bluff above Potomac River. Named for the Rev. Patrick Healy, president of university, 1874-82. 8 ext. photos (1969), 23 int. photos (1969), 9 photocopies of original plans, elevations and details (c. 1875-c. 1889); 42 data pages (1969). NR, JCL II

Old North Building (DC-170), on the Georgetown University Campus, 37th and O Sts., N.W. (Georgetown). Brick, seventeen-bay front, three-and-a-half stories on raised basement, central five-bay projecting pavilion with pediment, one-story wooden porch with balustraded deck, arched stone doorways with fanlights and side lights on porch and deck, oval window with quoins in pediment, belt courses separating floors. Begun 1792-93; oldest building remaining on Georgetown University campus. 4 ext. photos (1937, 1974*). JCL II

Georgetown Visitation Convent (DC-211), 1500 35th St., N.W. (Georgetown). Large complex of approx. 20 buildings including chapel, monastery, academy and educational buildings erected since the convent's establishment in 1799. Daughters of several presidents and other nationally prominent persons have been educated here. Chapel is stuccoed brick, approx. 36' (three-bay front) x 46', three stories, gable roof, Ionic pilasters support triangular pediment on facade; nave with gallery, crypt below. Built 1821, extensively altered. Academy building is brick, approx. 110' (five-bay front) x 85', three-and-a-half stories with another full story in mansard roof, bracketed cornice, paired dormers with arched heads, iron cresting, projecting pavilions in center of facades, elaborate entrance canopy and window head treatment. Built 1873; Norris G. Starkweather, architect. Small brick cabin on the property is 13'-6" x 23', one story, gable roof. Built 18th C. Probably overseer's house for Burleigh Plantation. 1 ext. photo of Academy Building (1968*); 31 data pages (1969*). JCL II

Gilman's Drug Store(Mathew Brady Studio) (DC-129), 627 Pennsylvania Ave., N.W. Brick, four-bay front, four stories, flat roof, arched windows with flanking colonnettes, shop front on first floor, western half of a double building, elaborate first floor interior with plaster ceiling and decorative shelves lining

wall. Built 1850s; original interiors destroyed 1967. Civil War
photographer Mathew Brady had studio on top three floors
1858-81. Gilman's Drug Store (established 1822) occupied first
floor until 1967. 1 ext. photo (1967*), 8 int. photos (1967*).

Godey Lime Kilns (DC-102), originally on the north bank of
the C & O Canal, the site is now the junction of Rock Creek and
Potomac Parkway and the Whitehurst Freeway. Rubble masonry with brick linings and arches. Operative 1864-1908, two
ovens demolished, 1964; ruins of remaining two ovens stabi-
lized, 1965-66. 3 sheets (1965, including plot plan, plan,
elevations, section); 1 ext. photo (1965), 4 photocopies (post
1907, 1910*, c. 1938); 4 data pages (1965). NR, JCL II

Golden Parrot Restaurant. See George Fraser House (DC-318),
NE. corner R and 20th Sts., N.W. at Connecticut Ave.

Goszler-Manogue House (DC-193), 1307 35th St., N.W.
(Georgetown). Brick row house, L-shaped, 22' (three-bay front)
x 40', two stories, gable roof, sawtooth brick cornice, side hall
plan. Built between 1794 and 1798; some interior alterations. 1
ext. photo (1968*); 19 data pages (1968*).

Goszler-Meem-Brown House (DC-204), 3412 O St., N.W.
(Georgetown). Brick row house, approx. 18' (three-bay front) x
29'-6", two stories with basement exposed in rear, gable roof,
side hall plan. Built between 1820 and 1830; renovated 1930. 1
ext. photo (1968*); 14 data pages (1968*).

Grace Church (Episcopal) (DC-101), 1041 Wisconsin Ave., N.W.
(Georgetown). Granite ashlar with sandstone trim, 38'-8"
(three-bay front) x approx. 70', two stories, gable roof with bell
cot, buttressed walls, projecting entrance vestibule, lancet
windows, open plan, auditorium on second floor, collar-braced
trusses, curved gallery, Gothic Revival style. Built 1866-67;
renovated 1922. Founded as a mission church for boatmen on C
& O Canal. 4 ext. photos (1966, 1967), 3 int. photos (1966); 15
data pages (1966). NR, JCL II

Gray, Horace, House (DC-79), 1601 I St., N.W. Brick, three-
and-a-half stories, gable roof, little ornamentation except for
flat brick arches above windows with contrasting-colored
corners, belt course at first floor sill level, narrow molded belt

course at second floor sill level, irregular fenestration. Built c. 1874; remodeled as Christian Science offices and reading room 1948; demolished 1960s. Home of Horace Gray, associate justice of Supreme Court, later home of John Barton Payne, chairman of the American Red Cross and secretary of the interior under President Wilson. 1 ext. photo (1959).

Grief. See Adams Memorial (DC-280), in section E, Rock Creek Cemetery, entrance at Webster St. and Rock Creek Church Rd., N.W.

Gutman-Wise Building (DC-117), 3140 M St., N.W. (Georgetown). Brick, 25' (front) x approx. 105', four stories, flat roof, commercial front on first floor, triple windows on three floors above, window area contained beneath segmental arch springing from pilasters, stamped tin cornice. Built c. 1909. 2 ext. photos (1966); 6 data pages (1966).

Halcyon House (Benjamin Stoddert House) (DC-69), 3400 Prospect St., N.W. (Georgetown). Brick, originally a three-part symmetrical mansion plan with 48' (three-bay front) x 36' main block and 16' x 24' flanking wings, main block two-and-a-half stories, wings have two low stories, gable roofs, central hall plan, paneled fireplace wall in NE. room. Built 1787 as a freestanding mansion overlooking the Potomac River by Benjamin Stoddert, first secretary of the navy; completely enclosed on the N. side by eccentric owner Albert Clemons, who worked on additions to the house for nearly 40 years, now a maze of apartments and unfinished rooms; original house still intact within the 20th C. shell. 3 ext. photos (1959, 1968*), photocopy of N. side before alterations (n.d.); 50 data pages (1959, 1969*); HABSI form (1959). NR, JCL II

Halliday, Henrietta M., House (Irish Chancery) (DC-261), 2234 Massachusetts Ave., N.W. corner of Massachusetts Ave. and Sheridan Circle, N.W. Concrete block and brick walls, limestone facing, irregular plan with two principal elevations, 49'-9" (three-bay Massachusetts Ave. entrance facade) x 23'-2" (one-bay Sheridan Circle facade), three-and-a-half stories, slate mansard roof, galvanized iron dormers, limestone dormer over entrance, rusticated ground floor, upper floors smooth with rusticated entrance bay and corners, second story windows have false balustraded and triangular pediments with supporting consoles and guillouche frieze, Louis XVI details, Adamesque

and Rococo interior details. Built 1908-9; William Penn
Cresson, architect; interiors altered 1911, Boal and Brown,
architects. Purchased by Irish Republic 1949. 2 ext. photos
(1972*), 4 int. photos (1970*), 3 photocopies of drawings
(1908*, 1911*); 21 data pages (1970-73*).

Hamburgh Village House (DC-10-6), 412 20th St., N.W. Frame,
20'-4" (three-bay front) x 28'-5" (including one-story rear
addition), two stories on raised basement, gambrel roof,
one-room and side hall plan. Built c. 1790; located in the old
town of Hamburgh, which was incorporated into the new
federal city; demolished 1935. 1 sheet (1934, including plans,
elevations, section, details); 3 ext. photos (1935); 2 data pages
(1936).

SOUTH ELEVATION   WEST ELEVATION   EAST ELEVATION   NORTH ELEVATION

Hamburgh Village House

Harnedy Row Houses (DC-206), 3617-21 Prospect St., N.W.
(Georgetown). Frame row houses, L-shaped, approx. 16'(two-
bay front) x 20', ell is 12' x 12', two stories, roof pitched
toward rear, simplified bracketed cornice. Built c. 1895 for
Mary Harnedy as rental housing; renovated c. 1954. 1 ext.
photo (1968); 13 data pages (1969).

Hauge, Christian, House (later Czechoslovakian Embassy, now
Embassy of the Federal Republic of Cameroon Chancery)
(DC-262), 2349 Massachusetts Ave., N.W. at intersecion of 24th
St. Brick with limestone facing, wedge-shaped, 67'-9" (Massachusetts Ave. facade) x 36'-8" (24th St.) x 65'-8" (depth
perpendicular to Ave.), three-and-a-half stories with additional
attic story under slate gable roof, S. bay is two stories, first
story was originally garage, iron roof cresting, 63'-high corner
tower with conical roof, gabled wall dormers with finials and
crockets, pierced balustrade, early 16th C. French details,
eclectic interiors with marble mantels and elaborate woodwork
and plasterwork. Built 1906-7; George Oakley Totten, architect;
upper floors damaged by fire 1933; one-story addition to NW.

built 1934; renovated 1972. Built as residence and legation offices by Christian Hauge, Norway's first minister to U.S.; served as diplomatic legation of Czechoslovakia 1930-69. 2 ext. photos (1970*), 5 int. photos (1970*), 2 ext. photocopies (1907*), 4 int. photocopies (c. 1945*), 3 photocopies of plans (1907*, 1972*); 17 data pages (1970-73*). JCL III

Haw, John Stoddert, House (DC-156), 2808 N St., N.W. (Georgetown). Brick row house, 30' front (three-bays), two-and-a-half stories on raised basement, gable roof, splayed wooden lintels, fanlighted entrance, side hall plan, interior entrance hall has fanlight similar to main door, interior woodwork remains. Built 1816-17; restored 1921. Home of several noted statesmen including Chester Bowles and George C. McGhee. 3 ext. photos (1937, 1942). NR, JCL II

Hedges, Nicholas, House (DC-160), 1069 Thomas Jefferson St., N.W. (Georgetown). Brick, 21'-2" (three-bay front) x 34'-4", addition extends to 55'-7", two-and-a-half stories, originally had shop on first floor and residence above, gabled roof, side hall plan, fine interior woodwork. Built sometime between 1815 and 1818; attributed to Trueman Beck; restored and rear addition added in 1941. 1 ext. photo (1967), 10 int. photos (1967), 3 ext. photocopies (1941), 1 photocopy of first floor plan (1967); 11 data pages (1967); HABSI form (1967). JCL III

Herron-Moxley House (DC-195), 1503 35th St., N.W. (Georgetown). Brick, approx. 45' square, three-bay front, two stories on raised basement, hipped roof, bracketed cornice, recessed entrance with Doric pilasters supporting entablature and pediment, covered porches on sides, two-story enclosed porch at rear, Greek Revival details, central hall plan, notable woodwork, marble mantels, gas chandeliers. Built 1853-54 for William T. Herron, a contractor. 1 ext. photo (1968*); 19 data pages (1967*).

Heurich, Christian, Mansion (Columbia Historical Society) (DC-292), 1307 New Hampshire Ave., N.W. Historic house museum. Brick with rusticated brownstone facing on principal facade, trapezoidal shape, 75' (New Hampshire Ave. facade) x 115' (Sunderland Pl. facade), three-and-a-half stories with partially exposed basement, mansard roof, round corner tower with conical roof rises above roofline, porte cochere at main entrance, several projecting bays ending in ornamental dormers,

Christian Heurich Mansion

Christian Heurich Mansion

one-story conservatory with cast copper facade, Romanesque Revival style, elaborate carving and plasterwork on interior, paneled dining room, original furnishings and fixtures preserved. Built 1892 for Christian Heurich, German immigrant, brewery owner and philanthropist; John Granville Meyers, architect; rear wing and carriage house by Appleton Clark. 1 sheet (1975, porte cochere detail); 6 ext. photos (1972*), 8 int. photos (1972*). NR, JCL II

High Street Bridge (Wisconsin Avenue Bridge) (DC-30), Wisconsin Ave., N.W. (formerly High St.) over C & O Canal

(Georgetown). Ashlar masonry, approx. 54' span, 50' roadbed, cast-iron railings. Built 1831 to span newly constructed C & O Canal. 2 sheets (1938-39, including plan, elevation, details).

Hillyer Place (DC-294), Parallel to, and halfway between, Q and R Sts., N.W., running one block between 20th and 21st Sts. Relatively undisturbed block of late 19th C. townhouses, two-and-a-half and three stories, side hall plans, most are brick, some have stone facing, central groups on each side of block were designed as a unit with mansard-fronted tile roofs, projecting bays and curved gables, 2030 was home of Washington architect Joseph Hornblower, it has four stories, austere flat facade with metal marquise and belt courses of egg-and-dart and meander moldings. The entire block presents a well-maintained period streetscape. Francis Poor House (Old Swiss Legation) at 20th St. end of block demolished 1972. Street named for Curtis J. Hillyer, California mine owner and real estate speculator, was originally carriage route to Hillyer's mansion. 6 ext. photos (1969*). JCL III

Holt, Dr. Henry C., House. See Jackson Hill (DC-21), National Zoological Park, off Adams Mill Rd. N. Of Ontario Pl., N.W.

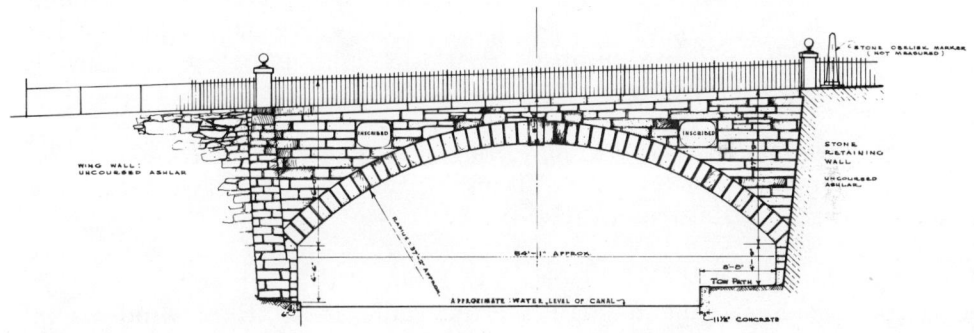

High Street Bridge

Holy Trinity Parish (Roman Catholic) (DC-201), 36th St. Between N and O Sts., N.W. (Georgetown). Complex includes original church (now Convent of Mercy), later church, and rectory, among other buildings. Original church is brick, 36' (three-bay front) x 110', (twelve bays), two stories, gable roof, 12'-square entrance tower in center of front elevation, octagonal frame belfry, bracketed modillion cornice. Built 1794; greatly altered and enlarged in early 19th C. Oldest place of

Catholic public worship in city, now used as convent. Present church is stucco over ashlar masonry, 64' (five-bay front) x 109', two stories, gable roof, giant order pedimented portico, projecting corner pavilions, modillion cornice, Classical Revival style, interior walls have giant order Ionic pilasters with full entablature and gilt trim. Built 1846-49. Rectory is brick, 38' (three-bay front) x 40', two-and-a-half stories on raised basement, concave mansard roof with dormers, bracketed cornice, entrance canopy supported by overscale wooden scrolls, central hall plan. Built 1869; Francis Stanton, architect; moved to present location 1917. 2 ext. photos of original church and rectory (1968*); 22 data pages (1968*).

Honeymoon House. See Thomas Law House (DC-20), 1252 6th St., S.W.

Hooe, James C., House (DC-263), 2230 Massachusetts Ave., N.W. Brick with limestone and terra-cotta trim, 28'-6" (three -bay facade) x 83'-2", three-and-a-half stories, mansard roof with metal cresting, wall dormers with shell motif in pediments, balustrade above corbeled cornice, stone quoins around windows and at corners, stone facing on first floor, drip moldings with bosses, central curved balcony with pierced stone railing, 16th C. Belgium details. Built 1907; George Oakley Totten, Jr., architect. 3 ext. photos (1970*, 1971*), photocopy of drawing (1909*), photocopy of plan (1972*); 2 data pages (1970-73*).

Hooper, Robert "King," House. See The Lindens (MASS-2-33), originally on Sylvan St., Danvers, Essex Co., Massachusetts; now at 2401 Kalorama Rd., N.W.

House (DC-17), 22 D St., S.E. Frame, 14'-2" (three-bay front) x 28'-3", two-and-a-half stories, gable roof, frieze windows in attic, facade has wooden siding channeled to resemble ashlar. Built early 19th C.; demolished 1937. 3 sheets (1937, including plans, elevations, details).

House (DC-183), 3015 Dumbarton Ave., N.W. (Georgetown). Frame, L-shaped, 23'-6" (three-bay front) x 65', two-and-a-half stories on raised basement, sloping roofs, wooden quoins, modillion cornice, oval attic windows with wooden floral grilles, convex denticulated window cornices, two-story wooden porch along rear ell, side hall plan. Rear portion of house appears to date from early 19th C., front block from mid 19th C., kitchen

3015 Dumbarton Ave., N.W. (Georgetown)

at rear is 20th C. addition. 3 ext. photos (1969), 1 int. photo (1969), photocopy of sketch plan (1969); 12 data pages (1968).

House (DC-236), 514 E St. at 6th St., N.W. Brick, 22′ (three-bay front) x 30′ (two bays), four stories above basement, flat roof, modified Roman Doric frontispiece entrance, wooden modillion cornice, side hall plan. Probably built c. 1840; grade level lowered c. 1871; minor alterations; demolished 1973. 1 ext. photo (1969); 1 data page (1969).

House (DC-136), 2029 E St., N.W. Federal style house, semicircular fanlighted doorway with pedimented frame, notable mantels. Built c. 1790; demolished. 3 photocopies of measured drawings of doorway and mantels (c. 1924*).

500 East Capitol St.

House (DC-331), 500 East Capitol St. Brick, four-bay front, rear ell, two stories plus a full story under slate mansard roof, central mansarded tower, bracketed modillion cornice, cast-iron hood molds and cresting. Probably built 1870s; shop front on first floor; demolished 1972. 2 ext. photos (1972*).

House (DC-54), 601 G St., S.W. Brick, five-bay front, two stories plus another story in concave slate mansard roof, brick window hoods, bracketed modillion cornice, one-story porches on two street sides. Built c. 1870; addition to W.; demolished during redevelopment of Southwest Washington. 1 ext. photo (1958).

House (DC-132), 1003 H St., N.W. Brick, three-bay front,
two-and-a-half stories on raised basement, horizontal attic
windows, denticulated cornice, main entrance framed by Doric
pilasters, entablature and pediment, side hall plan. Probably
built 1840s; demolished 1936. 2 ext. photos (1936), 1. int.
photo (1936).

House (DC-131), I St. between 18th and 19th Sts., N.W. Brick,
three-bay front, two-and-a-half stories on raised basement, low
hipped roof, denticulated cornice with egg-and-dart and meander moldings, horizontal frieze windows, pediment on consoles
above doorway, side hall plan. Built probably c. 1840;
demolished. 1 ext. photo (1937). Also see similar but larger
house: Alexander Ray House (DC-44), 1925 F St., N.W.

Houses (DC-15), 1000-2 Independence Ave., S.W. Brick double
house, 46'-8" (six-bay front) x 38'-1", two-and-a-half stories on
raised basement, gable roof, flat lintels with bull's-eye corner
blocks, entrance framed by engaged Tuscan columns and
entablature, side hall plans. Built c. 1840s; demolished. 3 sheets
(1936, including plans, elevations, details); 2 ext. photos
(1937).

House (DC-64), 2919 M St., N.W. (Georgetown). Stucco,
probably over brick, three-bay front, three stories, low gable
roof, commercial front on first floor. Probably built early 19th
C. 1 ext. photo (1935).

House (DC-32), 3111-13 M St., N.W. (Georgetown). Brick,
four-bay front, three-and-a-half stories, gable roof. Possibly
built late 18th C.; cornice, arched windows and first floor shop
front added mid 19th C.; demolished 1940. 1 ext. photo (1940,
showing demolition).

House (DC-33), 3115-17 M St., N.W. (Georgetown). Brick,
22'-5" front (four bays), three-and-a-half stories, gable roof,
splayed lintels with keystones, dormers have arched sash and
roofs, notable stairway and window trim. Built c. 1800; altered
with shop front on first floor; demolished 1940. 7 sheets
(1940*, including plans, elevations, details); 2 ext. photos
(1940, showing demolition); 2 data pages (1941).

House (DC-157), 2817 N St., N.W. (Georgetown). Frame with
clapboarding, three-bay front, two-and-a-half stories on raised

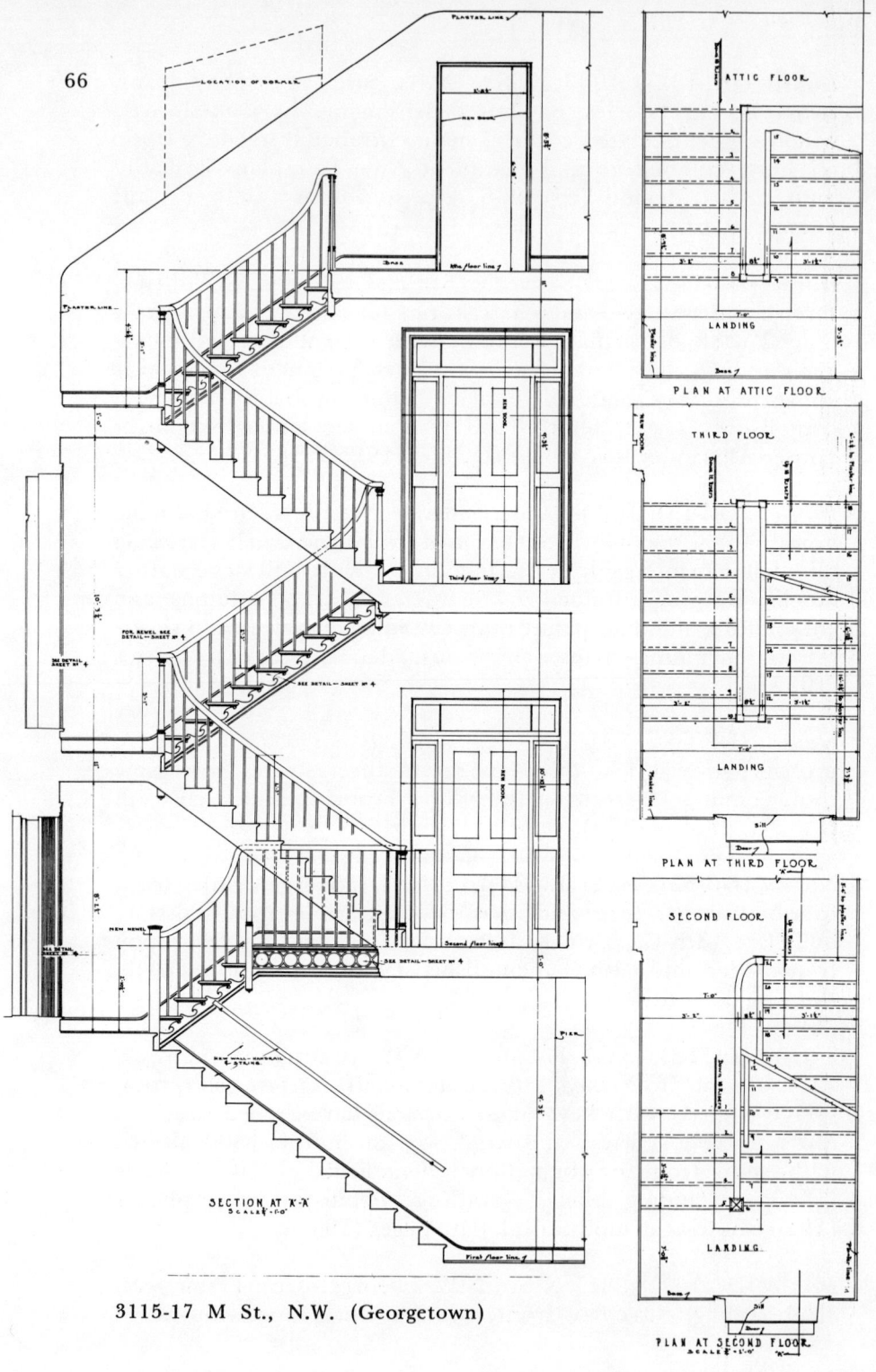

SECTION AT "X-X"
SCALE ½"=1'-0"

3115-17 M St., N.W. (Georgetown)

basement, gambrel roof, wooden entrance porch. Construction begun before 1800, gradually improved until 1819. 2 ext. photos (1937).

House (DC-27), 2411 Pennsylvania Ave., N.W. Brick, 26'-1" (four bays on ground floor, three bays above) x 38'-1", three-and-a-half stories on raised basement, gable roof, side hall plan, two half-gable rear additions attached to main house by frame connection. Probably built c. 1810; later door frame has modillion and bracketed cornice; demolished. 2 sheets (1936, including plans, elevations, details); 4 ext. photos (1936).

House (DC-126), 4437 Reservoir Rd., N.W. Hewn log, apparently built in two sections, one-and-a-half stories, gable roof, low shed-roofed addition across rear, one-story ell, gable ends and rear additions clapboarded; several small frame outbuildings. Built early 19th C.; restored. 4 ext. photos (1937).

House (DC-159), 1063 Thomas Jefferson St., N.W. (Georgetown). Brick, two-bay front, two-and-a-half stories, gable roof, arched entrance with fanlight, splayed lintels with keystones. Built early 19th C. 1 ext. photo (1937); HABSI form (1967).

House (DC-108), 1527-29 Wisconsin Ave., N.W. (Georgetown). Brick double building with passageway between, each unit approx. 24'-10" (three-bay front) x 65' (including rear ells), two-and-a-half stories, gable and pitched roofs, stone voussoir-and-keystone lintels, side hall plans. Built before 1837; 1529 later altered for commercial use and front elevation stuccoed to simulate ashlar. 3 ext. photos (1966); 7 data pages (1966).

House (now the Georgetown Club) (DC-109), 1530 Wisconsin Ave., N.W. (Georgetown). Frame with clapboarding and flush siding, side brick addition, 23'-2" (three-bay front) x 48'-2", two stories, low gable roof. Built c. 1845; two-story side brick addition 1965; interior extensively remodeled for private club use. 2 ext. photos (1966); 8 data pages (1966).

House (DC-226), 513 6th St., N.W. Brick, 26' (three-bay front) x 42', three-and-a-half stories above elevated basement, gable roof, entrance with semielliptical arch, fanlight, side lights, marble steps and stoop, ornamental iron rail, molded wooden cornice with consoles, side hall plan, open-string stair with ornamental brackets, arched opening with colonnettes in hall.

Probably built early 19th C. as two-and-a-half story structure; upper stories added perhaps c. 1860; grade level lowered c. 1871; modern alterations to basement. 3 ext. photos (1969), 2 int. photos (1969); 7 data pages (1969).

House (DC-237), 320 8th St., N.W. Brick, 20' front (three bays), four stories, gable roof, wooden lintels, simple wooden cornice above corbeled brick courses, side hall plan. Probably built before 1850; additions; first story remodeled for commercial use. 1 ext. photo (1969); 1 data page (1969).

House (DC-127), 723-25 20th St., N.W. Brick double house, four-bay front, three stories, low gable roof, brick denticulated cornice, attic windows in frieze, rusticated first floor, cast-iron balcony beneath second floor windows. Probably built c. 1840; demolished. 1 ext. photo (1937).

House (DC-337), SE. corner of 20th and I Sts., N.W. Brick, corner house of a row, entrance bay and semicircular three-windowed bow on facade, two-and-a-half stories on raised basement, mansard roof with decorative dormers. Built c. 1890; entrance changed to basement level; demolished 1971. 3 ext. photos during demolition (1971*).

House (DC-299), 2618 30th St., N.W. House incorporates the Romanesque double doorway from the Henry Adams Mansion on Lafayette Square, large arch once sheltered a bank of windows, grille from these windows now divided and placed beneath two upper floor windows, smaller arch reduced in size from original. Adams Mansion built 1885; H. H. Richardson, architect; demolished 1927 and fragments moved to present location. 6 ext. photos (1969*).

House Where Lincoln Died. See Petersen House (DC-165), 516 10th St., N.W.

Howard, Gen. Oliver O., House (now Howard University, Howard Hall) (DC-284), 607 Howard Pl., N.W. at W. entrance to Howard University campus. Painted hollow precast bricks, made on site, four-bay front, two-and-a-half stories on slightly raised stone basement, concave mansard roof with segmental dormers, one-and-a-half story rear wing, W. bay is a slightly projecting three-and-a-half-story mansarded tower with iron cresting, granite lintels with splayed voussoir-and-keystone motif, one-story wooden porches on front and rear, much of

2618 30th St., N.W.

Gen. Oliver O. Howard House

exterior ornament removed, main stairway and some original mantels remain. Built 1867-69 by Gen. O. O. Howard, commissioner of the Freedmen's Bureau and founder of Howard University; purchased by university 1909 and used as offices and classrooms since then. 1 ext. photo (1974*), 1 int. photo (1974*). NHL, JCL II

Hughes, Charles Evans, House (originally A. Clifford Barney House, now Union of Burma Chancery) (DC-278), 2223 R St., N.W. Stone facing, 50' facade (three bays), four stories, tiled mansard roof, overhanging eaves supported on projecting beams, rusticated first floor, second story windows are round-arched, third story windows have small paneled stone balconies on consoles, belt courses separate first and second, and third and fourth floors, glass and metal marquise, Mediterranean details. Built 1907; George Oakley Totten, architect. Purchased 1930 by Charles Evans Hughes, a leader of the Progressive movement, governor of New York, secretary of state, and chief justice of Supreme Court; acquired by Burmese Embassy after Hughes's death in 1948. 3 ext. photos (1974*). NHL, JCL III

Humble Service Station (DC-319), SW. corner 26th St. and Pennsylvania Ave., N.W. Brick, tile hipped roof with deck, S. end enclosed to form office, N. end supported by two brick columns, remainder is open and shelters gasoline pumps and driveways. Built 1930s; demolished 1970. 1 ext. photo (1970*).

Hurley, John, House (DC-200), 3619 O St., N.W. (Georgetown). Frame row house with stuccoed facade, approx. 16' (two-bay front) x 50', two stories, gable roof, bracketed modillion cornice, side hall plan. Built 1860s; interior remodeled for offices c. 1944. 1 ext. photo (1968*); 11 data pages (1968*).

Immaculate Conception Church (Roman Catholic) (DC-285), 1515 8th St., N.W., NE. corner of intersection of 8th and N Sts., N.W. Brick with stone trim, one story, gable roof with parapet, buttresses flanking tall lancet-arched windows, finials over buttresses project above parapet, Gothic Revival style. Built 1870-74; tower added 1904; exterior completed c. 1910; interior redecorated 1915 and 1940. Founded 1865 to serve undeveloped area N. of St. Patrick's Parish. Boy's school building to E. replaced original church and school building c. 1910. 1 ext. photo (1974*), 1 int. photo (1974*). JCL III

Indian Queen Hotel. See Brown's Marble Hotel (DC-322), 621 Pennsylvania Ave., N.W.

Humble Service Station

Indonesian Embassy. See Walsh-McLean House (DC-266), 2020 Massachusetts Ave., N.W.

Irish Chancery. See Henrietta M. Halliday House (DC-261), 2234 Massachusetts Ave., N.W.

Islamic Center, The. See Mosque (DC-286), 2551 Massachusetts Ave., N.W.

Jackson, Albert, House (DC-181), 1694 31st St., N.W. (Georgetown). Brick with elaborate wooden trim, irregular plan, 28' (at widest point) x approx. 65', two-and-half stories, intersecting gable roofs, carved wooden bargeboards with brackets, wooden window heads with interrupted cornice and raised floral design, three-sided one-story bay on front, entrance stoop along south side of front ell, late example of bargeboard cottage style. Built 1878-80; James H. McGill, architect; gingerbread entrance porch and chimney caps removed c. 1959 when house was remodeled. 1 ext. photo (1968), 1 int. photo (1968), 1 ext. photocopy (c. 1885), photocopy of sketch plan (1968); 6 data pages (1968, 1969).

Jackson Hill (Dr. Henry C. Holt House, later National Zoological Park, Administration Building) (DC-21), National Zoological Park, off Adams Mill Rd., N. of Ontario Pl., N.W. Stuccoed brick, five-part mansion plan with main block, wings and hyphens, approx. 89' x 58', originally one story on raised basement, gable roofs, denticulated cornice, projecting entrance vestibule. Built before 1827; traditionally associated with

Andrew Jackson and John Quincy Adams but stories unsubstantiated; residence of Dr. Henry Holt in mid 19th C.; house and land donated to newly formed National Zoo in 1890; substantially altered for Zoo offices in 1891, basement converted to entrance level, original interiors altered. 6 ext. photos (1937, 1974*); 2 data pages (1936). NR, JCL II

Jackson School (Public) (DC-244), SW. corner R St. and Avon Pl., N.W. (Georgetown). Brick, 70' (seven bays plus tower) x 80' (eleven-bay flank), two-and-a-half stories with partially exposed basement, hipped roof with deck, projecting five-sided tower at NW. corner with octagonal roof, slightly projecting gabled pavilions in center of three principal facades, bracketed cornice, central hall plan, four classrooms per floor, each with adjoining cloakroom. Built 1890. 2 ext. photos (1968, 1969), 6 int. photos (1969), photocopy of 1925 first floor plan; 10 data pages (1969).

Japanese Embassy (DC-264), 2516 Massachusetts Ave., N.W. Ashlar facing, 98'-10" (seven-bay front) x 78'-9" (E. elevation), two-and-a-half stories, hipped roof, three-bay projecting pedimented entrance pavilion, corner quoins, recessed arch above entrance, Georgian Revival style, two long wings flank main house and extend to sidewalk, wings joined by fence to form an enclosed court. Built 1931; Delano and Aldrich, architects. Designed as embassy with main house serving as residence and side wings as chancery buildings. 1 ext. photo (1971*); 2 int. photos (1971*); 2 data pages (1970-73*). NR, JCL II

Jackson School

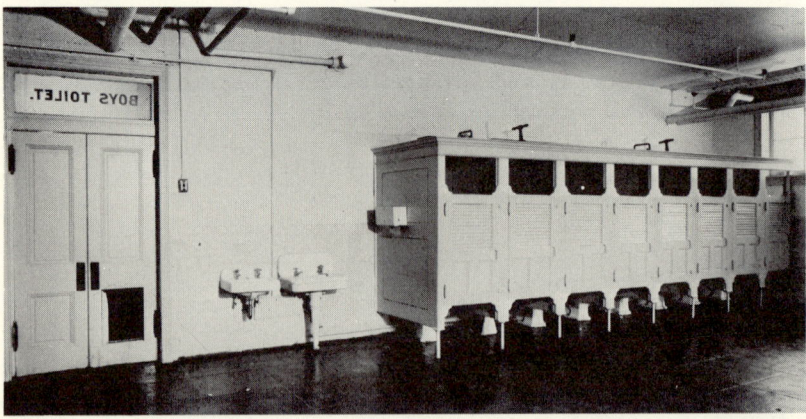

Capt. Joseph Johnson House

Johnson, Capt. Joseph, House (DC-3), 49 T St. at 1/2 St., S.W. (Buzzard's Point). Brick, 26'-1'' (three-bay front) x 32'-2'', two-and-a-half stories, gable roof with end parapets, side hall plan, keystoned arch spanning entrance hall. Built c. 1800; demolished 1930s. Capt. Johnson was a river and bay pilot. 2 sheets (1934, including plans, elevations, section, details); 2 ext. photos (1935), 2 int. photos (1935); 4 data pages (1936).

Kane, Daniel, House (DC-197), 1419 36th St., N.W. (Georgetown). Brick row house, 18' (three-bay front) x 32', two stories, pitched roof, simple modillion cornice. Built 1866; interior alterations; street grade raised 1890s, entrance now from areaway below street level. 1 ext. photo (1968*); 18 data pages (1969*).

Keep Building (DC-320), 801-5 Market Space (Pennsylvania Ave.), N.W. Brick building pair, each unit three bays, three-and-a-half stories, mansard roof, central bays have paired windows and gable at roofline, paneled pilaster strips with finial tops, patterned brickwork. Built c. 1880; two shop fronts altered; demolished 1968. 1 ext. photo (1967*).

Key, Francis Scott, House (DC-23), 3518 M St., N.W. (Georgetown). Brick with stone trim, 33'-7" (three-bay front) x 36'-11", two-and-a-half stories with basement exposed in rear, gable roof, splayed lintels with keystones, porch on S. overlooking terraced garden and Potomac River, side hall plan, kitchen and dining room in basement. Built 1802 by Thomas Clarke; occupied by Francis Scott Key, author of "Star Spangled Banner" 1805-30; Key added law office to W.; dismantled c. 1947 to make way for elevated expressway. 8 sheets (1933, 1940, including plans, elevations, details); 1 ext. photo (1935), 3 ext. photocopies (c. 1896, n.d.).

Key, Philip Barton, House. See Woodley (DC-52), 3000 Cathedral Ave., N.W.

King, Josiah W., House (Samuel McKean House) (DC-57), 528 17th St., N.W. Brick row house, two-bay front, three stories on full raised basement, flat roof, rear ell, triple windows at basement and first two floors, iron porch with curving stairs, porch roof and projecting bay are later additions. Built before 1814; demolished 1960. 1 ext. photo (1958); 1 data page (1959); HABSI form (1957).

Klingle House. See Linnean Hill (DC-11), 3545 Williamsburg Lane, N.W.; Rock Creek Park at intersection of Klingle Rd. and Porter St., N.W.

Knowles, William, House (DC-163), 1228 30th St., N.W. (Georgetown). Frame with clapboarding, approx. 22' (three-bay front) x approx. 46', two-and-a-half stories on raised basement, gable roof, two-column Doric porch with modillion cornice, small casement windows at attic level, side hall plan. Built after 1852 and before 1858. 3 ext. photos (1937, 1968), 2 int. photos (1968), photocopy of sketch plan (1968); 11 data pages (1968). JCL III

Kraemer, Charles, House (DC-283), 1841 Park Rd., N.W. Frame with narrow clapboarding, three-bay front, two-and-a-half stories, gable roof, slightly projecting pedimented entrance pavilion, Ionic pilasters at corners of house and pavilion, main entrance has elliptical fanlight and side lights, one-story semicircular entrance porch with balustraded deck, urns decorate balustrade, door to deck has scrolled pediment. Built 1906; Clement A. Didden & Son, architects; Boryer & Smith, builders. The finest

Charles Kraemer House

of several large Colonial Revival houses built in the Mount Pleasant area in the early 20th C. 2 ext. photos (1974*).

Lansburgh, Julius, Furniture Company. See Masonic Temple (DC-218), NW. corner F and 9th Sts., N.W.

Lansburgh's Department Store. See Commercial Building (DC-355), SE. corner E and 8th Sts., N.W.

Law, Thomas, House (Honeymoon House, now Tiber Island Center for Cultural and Community Activities) (DC-20), 1252 6th St., S.W.; NE. corner 6th and N Sts., S.W. Brick, 40' (five-bay front) x 31'-10", three stories on raised basement, modified hipped roof, first floor windows are round-headed and set in recessed arches, belt courses, splayed lintels with keystones, entrance has elliptical fanlight, cast-iron entrance porch and

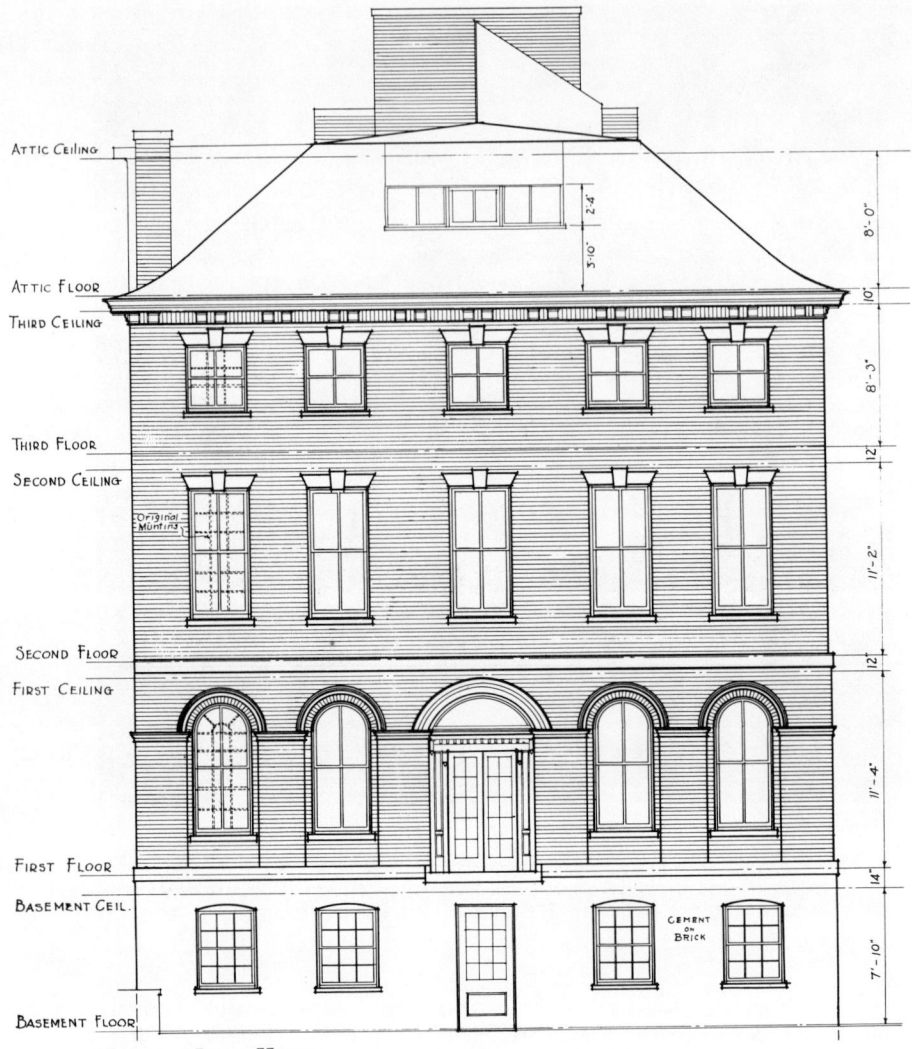

ATTIC CEILING

ATTIC FLOOR

THIRD CEILING

THIRD FLOOR

SECOND CEILING

Original
Muntins

SECOND FLOOR

FIRST CEILING

FIRST FLOOR

BASEMENT CEIL.

CEMENT
OR
BRICK

BASEMENT FLOOR

2'-4"

3'-10"

8'-0"

10'

8'-3"

12'

11'-2"

12'

11'-4"

14'

7'-10"

Thomas Law House

stairs of mid 19th C. date, central hall plan, interior largely altered. Built 1794-96; attributed to William Lovering, architect for the Greenleaf Syndicate. Leased in 1796 by Thomas Law, who lost a fortune made in India speculating on Washington real estate, and his bride Eliza Parke Custis Law, Martha Washington's granddaughter; served as a hotel in 1860s; used as a clinic after 1929; rehabilitated as part of Tiber Island urban renewal development 1965. 7 sheets (1936, including plans, elevations, details); 4 ext. photos (1936, 1937, 1974*). NR, JCL II

Layhman, Christopher, House. See Old Stone House (DC-2),
3051 M St., N.W. (Georgetown).

Le Droit Building (DC-212), 800-812 F St., N.W. Brick, U-shaped, 100' (seven-bay front) x 75' (five bays), four stories, flat roof, Corinthian frontispiece entrances, mullioned display windows, bracketed wooden entablature and cornice, second and third floor windows are triply grouped with brick hood molds; longitudinal hall plan. Built 1875 as shop and office building; James H. McGill, architect; storefront alterations on first floor. 3 ext. photos (1969), 1 int. photo (1969), 1 photocopy of drawing (conjectural restoration of block, 1969); 7 data pages (1969). NR, JCL II

Le Droit Building

Le Droit Park Area·Survey (DC-287), bounded by 2d and 7th Sts. and Florida Ave. and Elm St., N.W. Planned and developed as a residential subdivision of large free-standing houses and duplexes of related architectural design. Developed by Amzi L. Barber and Andrew Langdon on land purchased from Howard University in 1873. All houses designed by James H. McGill in style similar to A. J. Downing's country villas. 50 of original 64 houses remain. Between them are smaller brick and frame row houses of late 1880s and 1890s. Scene of early attempt at racial integration. Houses occupied by prominent D.C. and national figures up to present, including many noted black educators, poet Paul Lawrence Dunbar, and D.C. Mayor Walter Washing-

Le Droit Park Area Survey

ton. Anna J. Cooper founded Frelinghuysen University, an
adult education facility for working blacks, in her home at 201
T St. 1908 3d St.: 1 ext. detail of porch columns (1974*),
Carriage House, 314 U St.: 1 ext. photo (1974*), Double house,
603-05 U St.: 1 ext. photo (1974*), 1901 6th St.: 1 ext. photo
(1974*), 201 T St.: 3 ext. photos (1974*), 4 int. photos
(1974*). NR, JCL II

Lee, Thomas Sim, House (DC-65), 3001-3 M St., N.W.
(Georgetown). Brick, approx. 60' front (six bays), three-and-a-
half stories, gable roof, brick belt between second and third
floors, shop front on first floor. Built c. 1794 as city residence
for Thomas Sim Lee, former governor of Maryland; divided into
two houses c. 1805; street grade lowered exposing basement in
1870s; restored 1955, Howe, Foster, and Snyder, architects.
Preservation of this and adjacent building (DC-113) by Historic
Georgetown, Inc. spurred revitalization of Georgetown commercial area. 5 sheets (1974*, including plans, elevations); 1 ext.
photo (1935), 1 int. photo (1935, mantel detail). Also see
photos filed under Ross and Getty Building (DC-113). JCL II.

Thomas Sim Lee House

Lemon Building (DC-338), 1729 New York Ave., N.W. Brick, four-bay front, four-and-a-half stories, modified gable roof, bracketed cornice with rounded corners, arcuated fenestration, side oriels, intricate facade decoration of cast brick, iron grilles on first floor windows. Built 1891; Nathan C. Wyeth, architect; demolished 1971. 4 photogrammetric stereopairs (1970*).

Lewis, Edward Simon, House (erroneously known as Washington Lewis House) (DC-26), 456 N St., S.W. Brick, 31'-6" (three-bay front) x 39'-6", two-and-a-half stories on raised basement, gable roof, semicircular-arched entrance with fanlight, originally side hall plan, interior largely altered. Built c. 1817; renovated as part of Harbour Square urban renewal development project 1964-66. Onetime residence of newspaper correspondents Ernie Pyle and Lewis J. Heath. 3 sheets (1936, including plans, elevation, details); 4 ext. photos (1934, 1936, 1959, 1974*), 1 detail photo of lock (1936). NR, JCL II

Lewis, Washington, House. See Edward Simon Lewis House (DC-26), 456 N St., S.W.

Library of Congress (DC-351), NE. corner 1st St. and Independence Ave., S.E. New Hampshire granite, rectangle enclosing a cross which forms four inner courtyards, octagonal rotunda at crossing with copper dome and lantern, 470' (twenty-seven-bay front) x 340' (twenty-one-bays), lantern 195' high, projecting pavilions in center of front and rear facades and at each corner, ground floor treated as a fully exposed basement, above are two principal floors, third floor in pavilions and in rear wing, cellar below ground floor, hipped roofs, balustrade at eaves, granite is rock-faced on basement story, more finely dressed on first floor, smooth on second floor, first floor arched windows have ornamental keystones, pavilion keystones display 23 sculpted heads of races of mankind, second floor windows have alternating segmental and triangular pediments, pavilions have columns at second floor level, Italian Renaissance style, main entrance in central pavilion approached by grand terraced stairway, at base of terrace is *Court of Neptune* fountain by sculptor Roland Hinton Perry, interior features Italian white marble grand stairway, rotunda most lavishly decorated space, contains reading room and card catalog, surrounded by eight clustered piers, coffered dome, ornamented with paintings, mosaics, symbolic plaster groups, bronze portrait statues, smaller reading rooms on second floor in corner pavilions, arms

Library of Congress

of cross contain book stacks. Built 1888-97; Smithmeyer and
Pelz presented first plan; plans altered when construction put
under control of U.S. Army Corps of Engineers, Gen. Thomas
L. Casey, chief of engineers; Bernard R. Green, C.E., superintendent of construction; Paul Pelz served as architect 1889-92
and is primarily responsible for plan and exterior appearance;

82

Library of Congress

Edward Pearce Casey, architect from 1892-97, responsible for interior architectural features. Works of art commissioned from over 50 American painters and sculptors. 11 ext. photos (1974*, 1975*), 15 int. photos (1974*). NHL, JCL I

Lindens, The (Robert "King" Hooper House) (MASS-2-33), originally on Sylvan St., Danvers, Essex Co., Massachusetts; now at 2401 Kalorama Rd., N.W. Frame, principal facade cut and sanded to resemble rusticated ashlar, other three faces clapboarded, 57'-6" (five-bay front) x 42'-6", two-and-a-half stories on stone basement, gambrel roof with balustrade, denticulated cornice, steep one-bay central pediment supported on two-story fluted engaged Corinthian columns, simulated corner quoins and window voussoir, garden facade entrance has Ionic enframement with swan's neck pediment, central hall plan, notable interior woodwork, some mid 19th C. wallpaper, stenciled floors. One of finest examples of New England Georgian architecture. Built 1754 by wealthy loyalist merchant Robert "King" Hooper; residence of Gen. Gage, colonial governor of Massachusetts at outbreak of Revolution. Dismantled and moved to Washington, D.C., by Mr. and Mrs. George Maurice Morris in 1934; reerected 1935-37; Walter Macomber, restoration architect. 29 sheets (1934, before dismantling, including plot plan, plans, elevations, details, and garden plans); 6 ext. photos (1934), 16 int. photos (1934). Records filed under Massachusetts. NR, JCL II

Lingan, Gen. John, House. See Prospect House (DC-210), 3508 Prospect St., N.W. (Georgetown).

Linnean Hill (Joshua Peirce House, Klingle House) (DC-11), 3545 Williamsburg Lane, N.W.; Rock Creek Park near intersection of Klingle Rd. and Porter St., N.W. Granite rubble masonry, 67'-9" (five-bay front) x 22', two-and-a-half stories, gable roof, two-story projecting stone entrance porch with arched openings on ground floor, closed on second floor, applied corner buttresses, cast-iron porch and balcony on S. facade, central hall plan, some interior woodwork remaining, 6' x 4' fireplace with beehive oven, Pennsylvania German influence. Built 1823 by Joshua Peirce, son of builder of Peirce Mill and early horticulturist; side wing added 1843; became part of Rock Creek Park in 1890; restored by WPA 1937. Grounds once extensively landscaped, some original plantings remain; outbuildings include bank barn and two-story utility house and

The Lindens

corresponding potting shed built into rear terrace. 11 sheets (1936, including plans, elevations, section, details, one sheet of outbuildings); 8 ext. photos (1934, 1935), 2 int. photos (1934, 1935). NPS, JCL II

Litchfield, Grace Denio, House (DC-321), 2010 Massachusetts Ave., N.W. Brick, three-bay front, three-and-a-half stories on raised basement, modified hipped roof, severely plain facade, one-story balustraded sandstone entrance portico supported by paired composite columns, polygonal tower at SE. (rear) corner, stained-glass fanlight over entrance, projecting bay on E. side with decorative iron facing and supports. Built 1892; Hornblower and Marshall, architects; interior greatly altered; demolished 1969. Home of novelist / poet Grace D. Litchfield for 52 years. 4 ext. photos (1969*), 4 int. photos (1969*).

Lock Keeper's House (DC-36), SW. corner of 17th St. and Constitution Ave., N.W.; originally at the junction of the C & O Canal extension and the Washington City Canal. Fieldstone, 30' (three-bay front) x 18', one-and-a-half stories, gable roof, dormers begin in upper wall and extend through cornice. Built

1832-33; moved approx. 40' NW. in early 1930s when street widened; now used as a public restroom. 5 ext. photos (c. 1935). NPS, JCL II

Loeb Company Store. See Merchants and Mechanics Savings Bank (DC-239), NW. corner 7th and G Sts., N.W.

Logan Circle Area Survey (DC-339), intersection of Vermont and Rhode Island Aves. and 13th and P Sts., N.W. Circle was part of original plan for city of Washington by L'Enfant and Ellicott, originally named Iowa Circle, equestrian statue of Union General John A. Logan erected 1901. Residential area around circle built up from 1875 to 1900 in a variety of late 19th C. styles. Little demolition or exterior alteration has resulted in maintenance of period character. There are several large free-standing mansarded houses on the circle; most structures are row houses. 3 general views of circle (1970*), No. 1 and 2 Logan Circle: 3 ext. photos (1973*, 1974*), No. 4 Logan Circle: 1 ext. photo (1973*), No. 1500 13th St.: 2 ext. photos (1974*), No. 1502 13th St.: 2 ext. photos (1974*), No. 1314 Vermont Ave.: 1 ext. photo (1974*). 12 copies of composite photographs showing streetscapes on and around Logan Circle, including the 1500 block of 13th St., and the 1300 and 1500 blocks of Vermont Ave., and the 1200 and 1300 blocks of Rhode Island Ave. (1973*); 19 photocopies of line drawings of buildings on the same streets (1973*) (Photocopies of line drawings and composite photos courtesy of Turner Associates, Washington, D.C.). NR, JCL II

Logan Circle Area Survey, 1300 block of Vermont Ave., N.W.

Logan Circle Area Survey, 1500 13th St., N.W.

Longden House (DC-194), 1555 35th St., N.W. (Georgetown). Frame, 35' (three-bay front) x 20'-6", two stories above exposed basement, hipped roof, main entrance has side lights and fanlight, central hall plan. Built 1853 by George W. Longden, carpenter-builder; two-story 10' x 20' rear brick wing probably added late 19th C.; numerous changes since 1940 include distyle entrance porch, period mantels and woodwork. 1 ext. photo (1968*); 17 data pages (1967*).

Lovell, Joseph, House (Blair House) (DC-45), 1651 Pennsylvania Ave., N.W. Stuccoed brick, three-bay front, four stories on raised basement, flat roof, central hall. Built 1824 by Joseph Lovell, surgeon general of the army; originally two stories with gable roof; purchased 1837 by Francis Preston Blair, editor of the *Globe*; later home of Montgomery P. Blair, postmaster general under Lincoln; third story added before 1860; two-story one-bay addition to E. and fourth story added c. 1860; renovated 1931, Waldron Faulkner, architect. Residence of numerous cabinet officers; temporary presidential residence 1949-52 during White House remodeling; became official

government guest house for visiting dignitaries 1942; doorways
cut through joining house to adjacent Lee House (1653
Pennsylvania Ave.) in 1948. 2 ext. photos (1936); 7 data pages
(1961). JCL II

Lutz, John, House (formerly Female Benevolent Society, now
Aged Women's Home) (DC-105), 1255 Wisconsin Ave., N.W.
(Georgetown). Brick, approx. 20' (three-bay front) x 97'
(including rear ells), gable and pitched roofs, two stories, brick
cornice with dentils, cornice above entrance rests on ornate
consoles, modified side hall plans. Built in three stages: middle
section (flounder form) allegedly 1756; front section 1870; rear
ell 1872. 3 ext. photos (1966); 7 data pages (1966). JCL III

McCarthy-Sullivan House (DC-199), 3623 O St., N.W. (Georgetown). Frame, approx. 17'-6" square, two-bay front, two
stories, gable roof. Built early 1860s; concrete block addition at
rear, interiors altered. 1 ext. photo (1968*); 10 data pages
(1968*).

McCleery House (DC-162), 1068 30th St., N.W. (Georgetown).
Brick, 22'-5" (three-bay front) x 36'-3", originally two-and-a-
half stories, street level raised in 1831 making the house
one-and-a-half stories with areaway on east and fully exposed
basement on west, gabled roof, side hall plan, fine interior
details. Built c. 1800; restored 1952. 2 ext. photos (1967), 6
int. photos (1967), 1 copy of sketch plan (1967); 11 data pages
(1967). JCL III

McCormick Apartments (DC-265), 1785 Massachusetts Ave.,
N.W. Limestone facing, horizontal rustication on ground floor,
irregular shape, 79'-10" (five-bay Massachusetts Ave. facade) x
110'-10" (ten-bay 17th St. facade), four-and-a-half stories,
convex slate mansard roof, cast-iron railing at eaves, limestone
dormers with segmental and triangular pediments, rounded
corner entrance bay with triple windows, glass and iron
marquise, Louis XVI details, upper four floors had one
apartment per floor, first floor had entrance foyer and two
smaller apartments, elaborate interior plasterwork, marble
mantels. Built 1915-17; J. H. de Sibour, architect; interior
altered for offices. One of first luxury apartment buildings in
Washington; built for Stanley F. McCormick, son of Cyrus
McCormick. 1 ext. photo (1970*), 3 int. photos (1970*), 1
photocopy of drawing (1922*); 16 data pages (1970-73*). NR,
JCL II

Mackall Square (DC-164), 1633 29th St. between 28th, 29th, and R Sts., N.W. (Georgetown). Brick with frame ell, five-bay front, two stories on raised basement, gable roof, one-story wooden Ionic entrance portico with balustraded deck, elliptical fanlight, central hall plan. Main house built c. 1820 by Benjamin Mackall; three frame houses which form rear ell are 18th and early 19th C. 4 ext. photos (1937). JCL II

McKean, Samuel, House. See Josiah W. King House (DC-57), 528 17th St., N.W.

McLean, John R., House (DC-24), 1500 I St., N.W. Brick on raised stone basement, seven irregular bays on facade, two stories, hipped roof, decorative brick frieze under wide eaves, arched door surrounded by stone quoins, little exterior ornament, lavish interior designed for large-scale entertaining, columned conservatory with pool, banquet / ballroom which could seat 300, dining room with painted ceiling and monumental carved sideboard, theater with pipe organ, elaborate paneling, carved woodwork and plasterwork, Italian Renaissance Revival style. Original house built by Hamilton Fish; completely remodeled and enlarged in 1907; John Russell Pope, architect; demolished 1939. Home of John R. McLean, owner of the *Washington Post.* 7 ext. photos (1938), 18 int. photos (1938); 1 data page (1940).

Mackall Square

John R. McLean House, dining room sideboard

Madison, Dolley, House. See Richard Cutts House (DC-58), SE. corner H St. and Madison Pl., N.W.

Mahorney-Harrington House (DC-188), 1423 36th St., N.W. (Georgetown). Frame, approx. 20' (three-bay front) x 16', two stories, gable roof, bracketed modillion cornice, guttae beneath window sills, side hall plan. Built probably between 1821 and 1834; 16' x 20' brick addition to rear and interior alterations in late 1920s. 1 ext photo (1968*); 13 data pages (1969*).

Mahorney-O'Brian House (DC-198), 3522 P St., N.W. (Georgetown). Frame, approx. 16' (two-bay front) x 20', two stories, gable roof. Built between 1821 and 1832; modillion cornice and rear 16' x 16' addition added mid 19th C.; street grade raised 1890s, entrance now slightly below grade. 1 ext. photo (1968*); 15 data pages (1969*).

Mankins, William, House (DC-190), 1411 35th St., N.W. (Georgetown). Frame row house with stucco covering, approx. 21' (three-bay front) x 36', originally two stories, basement exposed as first floor when street level lowered, low gable roof, side hall plan. Built between 1834 and 1843; later alterations. 1 ext. photo (1968*); 19 data pages (1968*).

Manning, Edwin C., House (now Florida House, Headquarters of Florida State Society) (DC-330), 200 East Capitol St., NE. corner East Capitol and 2d St., N.E. Brick, 18'-6" x 47', two stories on raised basement, flat roof, three projecting full-height bays with champhered corners, large window openings, brick parapet, corbeled cornice, stained-glass transoms; typical of the late 19th C. row houses of Capitol Hill. Built 1891; C. C. Meads, builder; altered, renovated 1973. Owned by Robert R. Reynolds, isolationist senator from North Carolina and founder of the American Nationalist Party, who published the party paper, *American Vindicator,* in the house 1940-42. 3 ext. photos (1972*).

Edwin C. Manning House

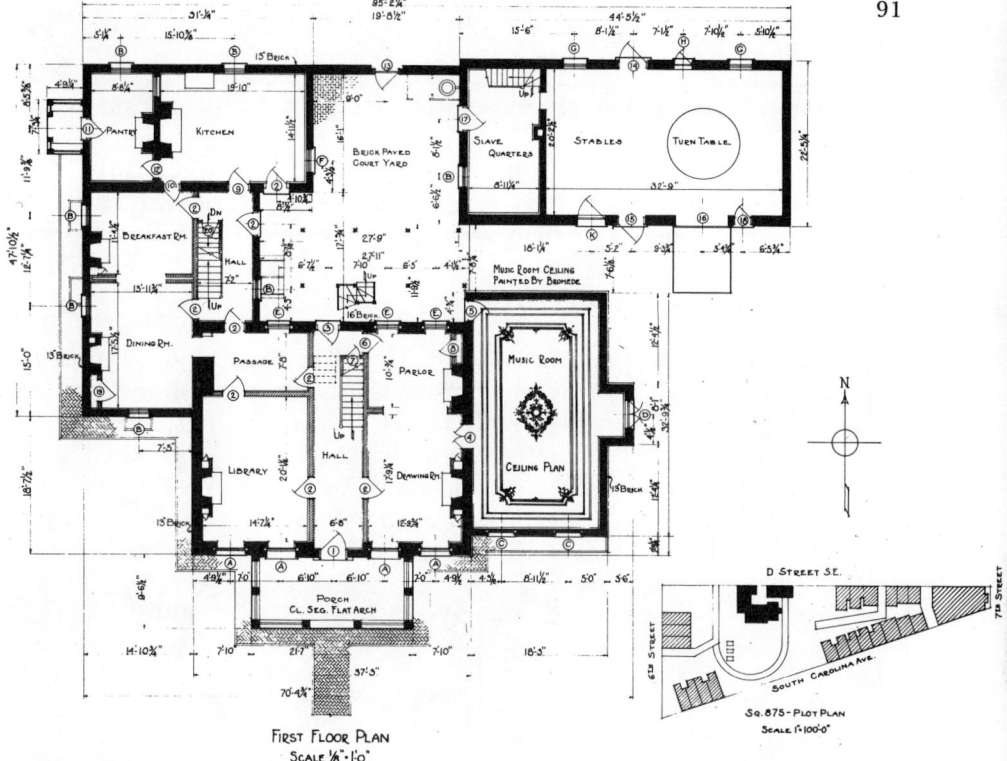

FIRST FLOOR PLAN
SCALE ⅛"-1'0"

The Maples

Maples, The (William Duncanson House, Maple Square, now Friendship House) (DC-5), 630 South Carolina Ave., S.E., entrance now at 619 D. St., S.E. Brick, main block 37' (five-bay front) x 32', two stories, gable roof, slightly projecting three-bay pedimented pavilion, bull's-eye window in pediment, central hall plan. Built 1795-96 for William Duncanson by architect / builder William Lovering; greatly enlarged and altered; ballroom decorated by Brumidi added to E. in 1856 by owner Sen. John M. Clayton, former secretary of state; further enlarged and marble mantels added after 1871 by author Emily Briggs; became Friendship House in 1936; completely renovated for institutional use by architect Horace Peaslee, ballroom replaced by side wing, former outbuildings renovated and joined to main house. 5 sheets (1934, including plans, elevations, section, details); 6 ext. photos (1935, before renovation), 9 int. photos (1935, 1936), photocopy of drawing of original doorway (c. 1924*); 1 data page (1935). NR, JCL II

Maple Square. See The Maples (DC-5), 630 South Carolina Ave., S.E.

Marceron, William, Building (DC-107), 1335 Wisconsin Ave., N.W. (Georgetown). Brick, truncated triangular shape, 34'-5" (three-bay arcuated front) x 9'-7" x 25'-9", one story with wide metal awnings on street elevations, flat roof with parapet, five-sided one-room plan with several small rear service rooms. Built c. 1890; later rear additions. 4 ext. photos (1966), 1 int. photo (1966); 5 data pages (1966).

Marcey-Payne Building (DC-106), 1321½–1325½ Wisconsin Ave., N.W. (Georgetown). Brick with cast-iron first floor facade, 48' (six-bay front) x approx. 50', three stories, flat roof, molded brick detailing, segmental-arched windows, party wall divides structure into two equal sections, interior largely unaltered. Built 1880s; windows of shop front altered. 4 ext. photos (1966), 1 ext. photocopy (1907); 9 data pages (1966).

Maret School (Private). See Woodley (DC-52), 3000 Cathedral Ave., N.W.

Masonic Temple (Also called Masonic Hall, now Julius Lansburgh Furniture Company) (DC-218), NW. corner of F and 9th Sts., N.W. Cast-iron veneer on brick, L-shaped plan, main portion 131'-5" (eight-bay front) x 51'-6" (three bays), four stories, flat roof, corner pilaster strips, paneled belt courses, pedimented windows, applied ornamental detail (largely removed), bold three-part cornice, facades of Italian Palace type. Built 1868-70; Cluss and Kammerhuber, architects; originally stores occupied ground floor, Masonic lodge rooms on third and fourth; interior remodeled c. 1921, inserting additional floor to convert to store building, first floor entirely altered. Cornerstone laid May 30, 1868, with President Andrew Johnson attending and marching in procession. 3 ext. photos (1969), 1 ext. photocopy (n.d.); 6 data pages (1969). NR, JCL II

Mason, John, House (DC-28), Theodore Roosevelt (originally Analostan) Island in Potomac River. Stuccoed rubble masonry, T-shaped, 87' x 59'-2", one story on raised basement, gable roof, windows of wing set in blind arches, Classical Revival style. Probably built between 1793 and 1796; abandoned and burned 1869; ruins destroyed after recording in 1936. Originally a summer estate with elaborately landscaped grounds, may

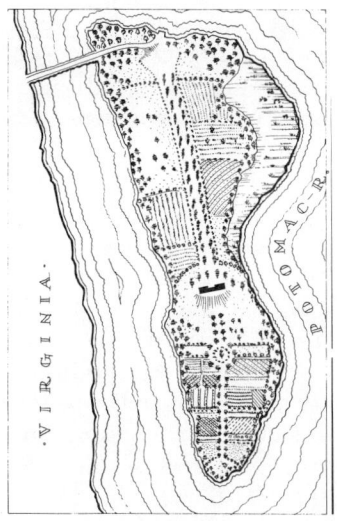

John Mason House

c. 1880-90 view

conjectural elevation

have been intended to have a symmetrical W. wing. 16 sheets (1936, including plot plan, plans, conjectural elevations, sections, details); 66 photos showing archeological excavation of ruins (1934-35, 1936 plus keyed plan of camera locations), 8 photocopies of sketches, maps, old photos (n.d., c. 1880-90, 1905, 1910), 4 photocopies of drawings (1918); 23 data pages (c. 1936).

Mason, John Thomson, House (Quality Hill, Worthington House) (DC-167), 3425 Prospect St., N.W. (Georgetown). Brick, L-shaped, approx. 56' (five-bay front) x 42', 40'-6" x 18' ell, two-and-a-half stories, gable roof with dormers, modillion cornice, fanlighted entrance in paneled reveal, fluted pilasters and triangular pediment, flat-arched lintels with voussoir and molded keystones, central hall plan, notable interior woodwork, finely carved Federal mantels. Built 1797-98 for John T. Mason; restored 1942. One of the finest freestanding 18th C. houses in Georgetown. 3 ext. photos (1936, 1968*), 4 int. photos (1968*), 32 data pages (1968*). NR, JCL II

Maury, John, House. See Charles Wiltberger House (DC-4), 302 C St., N.W.

Meigs, Gen. Montgomery C., House (DC-50), 1239 Vermont Ave., N.W., SE. corner Vermont Ave. and N St., N.W. Stuccoed brick, three-bay front, two stories with additional story in slate mansard roof, enriched modillion cornice above dentil course, first floor stuccoed to simulate rusticated masonry, corner quoins, classical medallions between second floor windows, one-story demioctagonal bay, central hall, curving stair, finely carved wooden mantel in parlor, fireproof construction. Built c. 1870; Montgomery C. Meigs, architect; additions and alterations; demolished. Meigs was quartermaster general during Civil War, he also designed and / or supervised construction of a number of major buildings and engineering structures in Washington and vicinity, including the Pension Building and Washington Aqueduct. 2 ext. photos (1958), 2 int. photos (1958); 1 data page (1959); HABSI form (1959).

Memorial Continental Hall (National Society of the Daughters of the American Revolution, Headquarters and Museum) (DC-282), 1776 D St., N.W. Brick and concrete with Vermont marble facing, three stories on raised basement, third story is recessed above cornice line and concealed behind balustrade, low mansard roof, projecting corner pavilions with quoins,

monumental porticoes on three street facades, principal portico
projects over driveway to form porte cochere for main entrance,
Classical Revival style. Built 1904-10 as national headquarters
and assembly hall for DAR; Edward Pearce Casey, architect;
assembly room was the site of the Washington Conference in
1921, a pioneering effort at international arms limitation; this
hall converted to a library 1949. 1 ext. photo (1974*), 1 int.
photo (1974*). NHL, JCL III

Merchants and Mechanics Savings Bank (now Loeb Co. Store)
(DC-239), NW. corner 7th and G Sts., N.W. Brick, 20' (three
bays) x 70' (seven bays), three stories plus one story in dormered
mansard roof, ornamental cast-iron trim. Built c. 1865; first
story remodeled. 1 ext. photo (1969); 1 data page (1969).

Methodist Episcopal Parsonage House (DC-176), 1221 28th St.,
N.W. (Georgetown). Frame row house, L-shaped, 25' (three-bay
front) x 43' (including ell), two-and-a-half stories with basement, gable roof, side hall plan. Built c. 1818-19 by Henry
Foxhall, who bequeathed it to the Methodist Episcopal Church
as a parsonage. 2 ext. photos (1969), photocopy of sketch plan
(1968); 11 data pages (1968, 1969).

Metropolitan African Methodist Episopal Church (DC-352),
1518 M St., N.W. Red brick with granite trim, 80' (five uneven
bays) x 120', two stories with basement, gallery in auditorium,
gable roof, projecting central door with lancet enframement,
lancet windows in various groupings, square towers with applied
buttresses at corners of facade, buttresses terminate in pinnacles
above roofline, original interior survives, auditorium on second
floor, semicircular seating, Gothic details. Built 1886; Samuel
G.T. Morsell, architect. One of the largest Negro churches in the
country when built. 1 ext. photo (1974*), 1 int. photo
(1974*). NR, JCL II·

Metropolitan Hotel. See Brown's Marble Hotel (DC-322), 621
Pennsylvania Ave., N.W.

Michler Place (DC-340), N. side of F St. between 17th and 18th
Sts., N.W. (Nos. 1739-51 remain). Row of twelve brick houses
of unified design, originally two-and-a-half and three-and-a-half
stories with dormered mansard roofs, two units at each end and
two central units had an additional story, houses separated by
large scroll motif at roofline, decorative window hoods,

Metropolitan African Methodist Episopal Church

doorways had entablatures on scrolled consoles. Built between 1870 and 1876 by "Boss" Alexander Shepherd; lowering of street grade exposed basement floors of most buildings which were converted to commercial fronts; greatly altered over the years, much of decorative detail lost; eastern five houses demolished 1965 and after. Named for Gen. N. Michler, superintendent of public buildings and grounds 1867-71, first man to hold that office after authority was placed under Army Corps of Engineers. 2 ext. photos (1974*).

Miller, Benjamin, House (DC-247), 1524 28th St., N.W. (Georgetown). Frame, L-shaped, 30' (three-bay front) x 61', two stories, gable roof, end chimneys, one-story Greek Revival porch has fluted Doric columns supporting entablature and pediment, central hall plan. Built c. 1843; probably by Benjamin Miller, master carpenter and superintendent of construction for the Potomac Aqueduct. 1 ext. photo (1968), photocopy of sketch plan (1968); 13 data pages (1969). JCL III

Miller House (Argyle Terrace) (DC-275), 2201 Massachusetts Ave., N.W. Roman brick with stone trim, irregular plan, 66' x

34', three-and-a-half stories on raised stone basement, three-bay entrance facade is flanked by two-bay bows, bows have conical roofs, main roof is mansard, random rustication on basement, one-story stone entrance porch with paneled balustrade and urn decoration, double stone stairway approaches porch, splayed rusticated lintels and keystones on upper floors, wide plain stone friezes above first and third floors, swag panels on bows, stone dormers with scroll pediments, large gabled central dormer, notable interior woodwork with nautical motifs, contemporary mansarded garage to NE. built expressly for an automobile. Built 1900-1901; Paul J. Pelz, architect; converted to rooming house. 2 ext. photos (1970*), 3 int. photos (1970*), photocopy of plan (1973*); 19 data pages (1970-73*).

Moore, Clarence, House (Canadian Chancery) (DC-267), 1746 Massachusetts Ave., N.W. Roman brick, rusticated limestone facing on ground floor, limestone trim above, 59' (three-bay front) x 101', four-and-a-half stories, mansard roof, arched windows on second floor with decorative keystones and limestone balcony, third floor windows have iron balconies, Tuscan cornice separates third and fourth floors, balustrade at eaves, Louis XV style, eclectic interior with elaborate woodwork and plasterwork in 16th, 17th, and 18th C. French and

Michler Place

Clarence Moore House

Original drawing, 1906

English motifs. Built 1906-9; J. H. de Sibour, architect;
four-story addition to W. 1917. Quarters of the Canadian
diplomatic mission since it was established in 1927. 1 ext.
photo (1970*), 8 int. photos (1972*), 1 ext. photocopy (c.
1915*), 2 photocopies of drawings (1906*, 1908*), photocopy
of plan (1973*); 21 data pages (1970-73*). NR, JCL II

Moran, Francis B., House (Pakistani Chancery) (DC-268), 2315
Massachusetts Ave., N.W. at intersection with Decatur Pl.
Stuccoed brick with limestone and terra-cotta details, triangular
shape with three-bay circular tower at apex, 80' (Massachusetts
Ave. facade) x 86' (Decatur Pl. facade) x 70', three-and-a-half
stories with additional attic story under slate mansard roof,
rusticated first floor, corner quoins on upper floors, two-story
fluted Corinthian pilasters flank central bay on Massachusetts
Ave., segmental-arched dormers, applied swags, cartouches, and
panels with classical figures, balustraded balcony on circular
tower. Built 1909; George Oakley Totten, architect. 3 ext.
photos (1970*, 1971*), 1 int. photocopy (1915*), 3 photocopies of drawings (1908*); 3 data pages (1970-73*).

Mosque (The Islamic Center) (DC-286), 2551 Massachusetts
Ave., N.W. Steel frame with limestone facing, building complex
consists of mosque with open forecourt and two wings joined
by double arcade which encloses court on front, mosque has
open plan with a single 160'-tall minaret, low central dome,
battlemented eaves, interior features Turkish tile wainscoting
and mihrab, Persian rugs, inlain pulpit, pierced stone windows,
ornamental carved plaster, mosaics, decorative Arabic inscrip-
tions; building is placed at angle to street so mihrab is facing
Mecca; basement has modern auditorium; one wing houses
library and museum of Islamic Center, other wing houses offices
and residence of director of center. Cornerstone laid 1949,
building dedicated by President Eisenhower 1957; plans drawn
by Egyptian Ministry of WAKFS (Works); American architects
were Irwin S. Porter and Sons; builder was Joseph Howar, a
Washington Moslem; artisans imported to execute decorative
work. Project sponsored by diplomatic mission heads from
Moslem countries to promote international understanding. 4
ext. photos (1972*).

Mount Vernon Theater (DC-254), 918 9th St., N.W. Stuccoed
brick, 21' x 105', one story, flat roof, entrance arch of pressed
metal studded with light bulbs, curving parapet with raised

Mosque (The Islamic Center)

initials *M* and *V*. Built 1910; A. B. Mullett and Co., architects; ceased to be a theater 1913; front and interior altered. A rare surviving example of the nickelodeon, earliest type of building designed expressly for showing motion pictures. 2 sheets (1969*, including map, elevation); 5 ext. photos (1969*); 14 data pages (1970*).

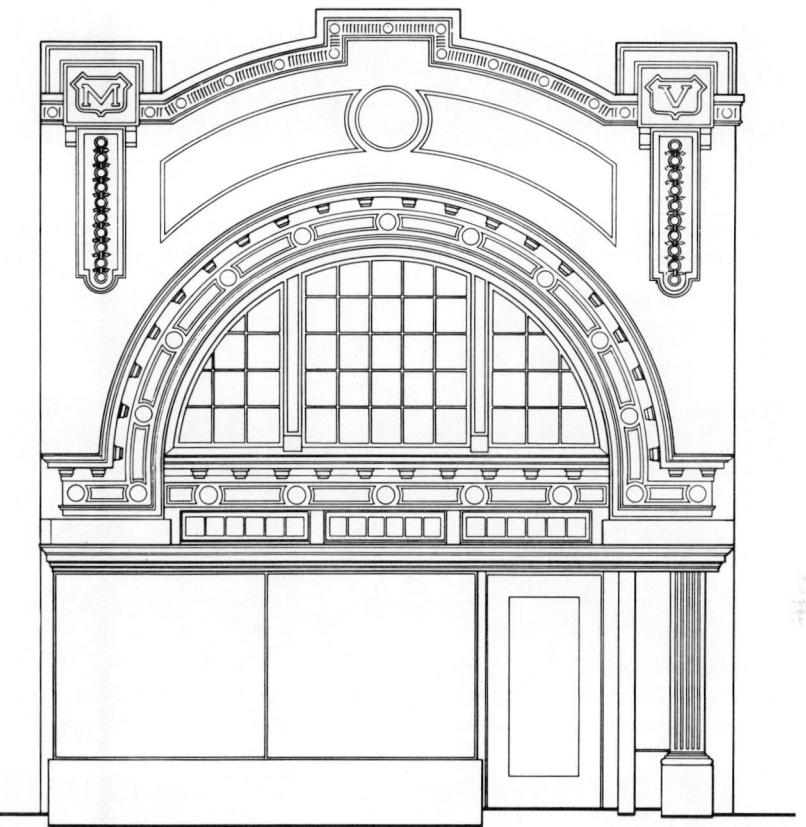

Mount Vernon Theater

Mount Zion United Methodist Church (DC-242), 1334 29th St., N.W. (Georgetown). Brick, 50' (three-bay front) x 75', two stories, gable roof, two slightly projecting pseudotowers with flat caps flanking facade, central portion contains entrance door below grouping of three lancet windows, large lecture room and Sunday school rooms on first floor, sanctuary with U-shaped balcony on second floor, pressed metal ceiling in sanctuary. Built 1876-84; 15' addition to rear 1904. Reputed to be the oldest Negro church in the District of Columbia and also to have been a stop on the Underground Railroad. 1 ext. photo (1968), 3 int. photos (1969), photocopy of c. 1969 plans showing proposed alterations; 17 data pages (1969).

Mountz, John, House (Eagle house) (DC-18), 3016 M St., N.W. (Georgetown). Brick, approx. 20'-6" front (three bays), three-and-a-half stories, gable roof, two doors on ground floor, one

Mount Zion United Methodist Church

with flat arch and straight transom, one with segmental arch and fanlight, windows have splayed lintels with cast-iron stars, keystones of doors and windows decorated with carved eagles, cast-iron second floor balcony. Built c. 1795; demolished 1942. 4 sheets (1937, including elevation and details); 3 ext. photos (1935, 1937).

National Archives (DC-296), Constitution Ave. between 7th and 9th Sts., N.W. Steel skeleton with granite base and limestone facing, approx. 330' x 206', five stories of office space and 21 tiers of document storage, flat roof, facades have applied rows of Corinthian columns, monumental projecting Corinthian porticoes on N. and S., massive attic rises above entablature, interior has 75' high semicircular exhibit hall. Houses most important U.S. government documents. Built 1931-37; John Russell Pope, architect; sculpture by James Earle Fraser, Robert Aitken, and Adolph Weinman. 1 ext. photo of sculpture (1971*). NR, JCL II

National Bank of Washington (now National Bank of Washington, Washington Branch) (DC-223), 301 7th St., N.W., intersection of Indiana Ave., 7th, and C Sts., N.W. Rock-faced marble ashlar, smooth tooled trim, rock-faced granite base, polygonal

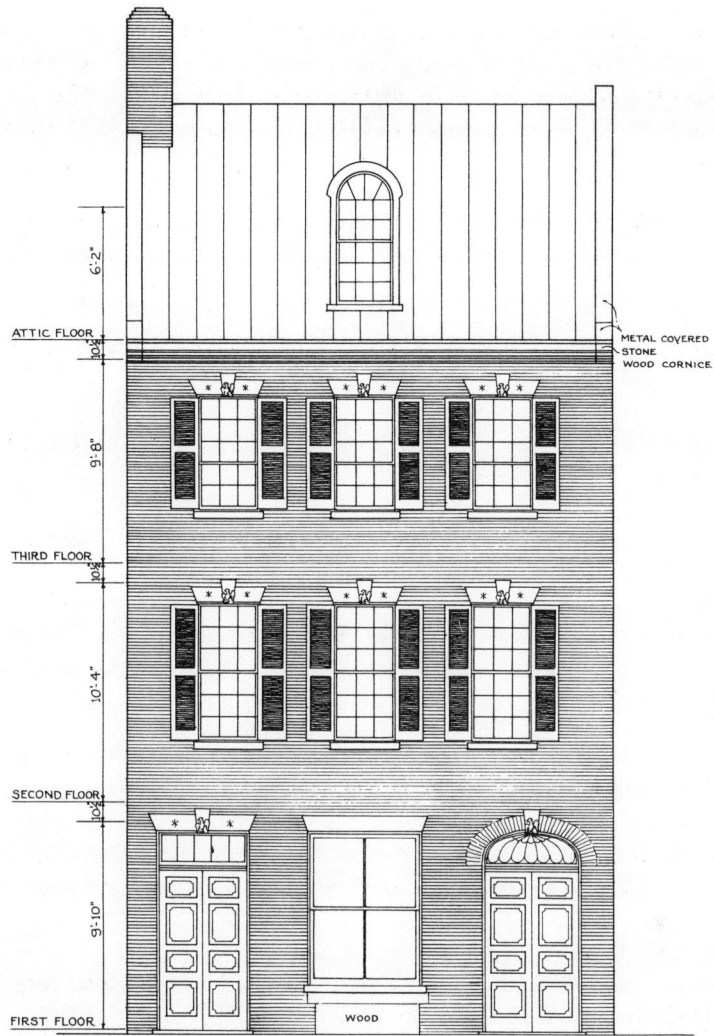

6'-2"

ATTIC FLOOR

METAL COVERED
STONE
WOOD CORNICE.

9'-8"

THIRD FLOOR

10'-4"

SECOND FLOOR

9'-10"

FIRST FLOOR

WOOD

John Mountz House

shape, 108'-9", 39'-11" and 109'-2" frontages, two stories plus
mezzanine, hipped roof with ornamental dormers, entrance
porch with semicircular arch of three molded orders, clustered
colonnettes, carved foliated impost and capitals, other relief
carvings of Byzantine character, windows with mullion and
transom bars, ornamental wrought-iron grilles, main banking
room on first floor, offices on mezzanine and second floors,
notable ornamental plasterwork, cherry paneling, mantelpieces,

floor construction arched masonry panels between iron joists. Built 1889 (original building comprises western 80' of present structure); addition to E. in matching style built c. 1922. 2 ext. photos (1967), 4 int. photos (1969); 10 data pages (1969). NR, JCL II

National Bank of Washington, Georgetown Branch. See Potomac Savings Bank (DC-323), 1200 Wisconsin Ave., N.W. (Georgetown).

National Collection of Fine Arts. See Patent Office (DC-130), bounded by 7th, 9th, F, and G Sts., N.W.

National Firefighting Museum. See Bank of Columbia (DC-119), 3210 M St., N.W. (Georgetown).

National Portrait Gallery. See Patent Office (DC-130), bounded by 7th, 9th, F, and G Sts., N.W.

National Presbyterian Church. See Church of the Covenant (DC-140), SE. corner 18th and N Sts., N.W., at Connecticut Ave.

National Trust for Historic Preservation. See Decatur House (DC-16), 748 Jackson Pl., N.W.

National War College. See Army War College (DC-277), Fort Leslie J. McNair, entrance on P St. between 3d and 4th Sts., S.W.

National Zoological Park, Administration Building. See Jackson Hill (DC-21), National Zoological Park, off Adams Mill Rd. N. of Ontario Pl., N.W.

Naval Observatory, Old (U.S. Navy Bureau of Medicine and Surgery, Potomac Annex, Building no. 2) (DC-341), entrance to grounds at 23d and E Sts., N.W. Brick, two stories, flat roof with observatory dome, Doric pilasters, windows and door have entablatures supported on consoles. Built 1843; wings added to E., W. and S. before 1893; circular building to house additional telescope added at end of S. wing 1873; second floors of wings added after 1880. One of the federal government's earliest and most important scientific ventures. First superintendent of the observatory, Matthew F. Maury, gained international fame for his oceanographic and astronomical research. Observatory moved to present location on Massachusetts Ave. in 1880s. 1 ext. photo (1974*), 1 int. photo (1974*). NHL, JCL II

Nineteenth Street Baptist Church (DC-357), SW. corner 19th and I Sts., N.W. Red pressed brick, three-bay front with entrance bay flanked by mansared towers with chamfered corners, two stories, gable roof, low rear tower at NW. corner, side bays separated by buttresses, arched windows with brick hoods on second floor, stained glass, round window in central gable, auditorium on first floor, sanctuary above. Built 1871; remodeled 1917; sold by congregation 1975; to be demolished. Oldest Black Baptist church in Washington. Site originally occupied by First Baptist Church, a mixed congregation founded in 1802; White members moved to new church in 1833; first Black congregation formally organized in 1839. Scene of important programs in Black education. 5 ext. photos (1975*). JCL III

Nordlinger Building (DC-116), 3128 M St., N.W. (Georgetown). Brick, 20'-6" (four-bay front) approx. 75', three-and-a-half stories, flat roof, molded brick trim, arcuated facade with separating pilasters, stamped tin modillion cornice with central pediment. Built late 19th C.; shop front and interiors altered. 2 ext. photos (1966); 5 data pages (1966).

Northern Market (O Street Market) (DC-342), NW. corner 7th and O Sts., N.W. Brick, five-bay front, six-bay flank, gable roof with monitor, large square tower with pyramidal roof at SE. corner, corbeled cornice, one-story open plan, office space in second story of tower. Built c. 1888; metal shed roof along S. and E. sides a later addition. After controversial demolition of Northern Liberties Market by "Boss" Shepherd in 1872, some of merchants set up temporary stalls between 6th, 7th, O, and P Sts., they formed Northern Market Co. and purchased land for present building. 2 ext. photos (1974*). JCL III

Oak Hill (Red Wood, Robert French House) (DC-42), Connecticut Ave., N.W., opposite present entrance to National Zoological Park. Frame with clapboarding, five-bay front, two-and-a--half stories on raised stone basement, gable roof with large square cupola, two-floored porch across entire front, central hall plan. Probably build c. 1819 by a Dr. Boyle, purchased 1853 by Capt. Edmund French III and owned by him for many

Oak Hill, c. 1900 view

years; numerous wings and additions including elevated square tower; demolished early 20th C. 1 ext. photocopy (c. 1900).

Oak Hill Cemetery

Chapel (DC-172), 350′ NE. of cemetery entrance gates at 3001 R St., N.W. (Georgetown). Potomac gneiss in random ashlar with red sandstone trim, 23′-2″ x 41′-2″ (four-bay flank), one story, gable roof, rose window above door in W. (front) elevation, large lancet-arched stained-glass window with sandstone tracery on E. elevation, similar smaller windows on side elevations separated by stepped buttresses, bell cot at peak of ridge on W., Gothic finial on E., Gothic Revival style, paneled ceiling with exposed beams. Built 1850; James Renwick, architect. Cemetery land, gatehouse, and chapel donated by philanthropist W. W. Corcoran. 14 sheets (1967, including plot plan, plan, elevations, sections, details); 5 ext. photos (1969), 2 int. photos (1969); 9 data pages (1969). NR, JCL II

Gatehouse (DC-249), 3001 R St., N.W. (Georgetown). Brick with sandstone trim, irregular plan, 40′ x 68′, office block is three stories, attached residence to W. is two stories, gable roofs with overhanging bracketed eaves, three-story tower at SE. corner with arcaded bell housing, angle buttresses, arched

Oak Hill Cemetery Gatehouse

windows with sandstone hoods on office block, Italianate and Gothic Revival details. Built 1850-53; attributed to Capt. George de la Roche; major alterations c. 1867 when office portion raised from two to three stories and a two-story dining room wing added; subsequent minor additions. Land, gatehouse, and chapel donated by philanthropist W. W. Corcoran. 3 ext. photos (1968, 1969), 1 int. photo (1969); 15 data pages (1969).

Occidental Hotel and Restaurant (DC-325), 1411-13 Pennsylvania Ave., N.W. Steel frame, brick simulating rusticated ashlar, stuccoed on first two floors, two-bay front, U-shaped with lightwell, eight stories, mansard-fronted roof, iron balconies on consoles, iron grilles, wall dormers, Beaux Arts style. Built 1903; Frank N. Carver, architect; two-bay, two-story addition to W. built 1914; A. B. Mullett and Co., architects. 1 ext. photo (1967*).

Octagon, The (Col. John Tayloe House, American Institute of Architects Headquarters) (DC-25), 1799 New York Ave., N.W. Historic house museum. Brick with sandstone trim, irregular hexagonal shape with projecting semicircular entrance bay, three stories on raised basement, low hipped roof, one-story Ionic porch, belt course, recessed panels between floors, circular vestibule, central three-story stairwell, elaborate plasterwork, coade stone mantels. Excellent and innovative example of Federal style domestic architecture. Built 1798-1800; William Thornton, architect; original flat roof replaced c. 1825; became headquarters of the AIA in 1902; major restorations 1947-56 and 1968-70, J. E. Fauber, Jr., restoration architect; now used as historic house museum and gallery. Served as executive mansion for a year after British burned the White House in 1814; Treaty of Ghent signed in circular room on second floor. 8 ext. photos (1936, 1971*), 20 int. photos (1936, 1971*), 2 ext. photocopies (1927*). NHL, JCL I

> *Stable* (American Institute of Architects Library) (DC-336), rear of 1799 New York Ave., N.W. Brick, approx. 65′ x 21′, two stories, flat, roof, slightly projecting central bay with two arched carriage doors, fenestration of side bays contained in large recessed arches. Built c. 1800; remodeled into AIA Library, 1953; Howe, Foster & Snyder, architects; demolished 1971. 1 ext. photocopy (c. 1927), 2 photocopies of drawings (c. 1927); 3 data pages (1965).

Octagonal House. See Bebb House (DC-13), 1830 Phelps Pl., N.W.

Old Ebbitt Grill. See Commercial Building (DC-315), 1427 F St., N.W.

Old Soldiers Home. See U.S. Soldiers Home (DC-353), entrance at Rock Creek Church Rd. and Upshur St., N.W.

Old Stone House (Christopher Layhman House) (DC-2), 3051 M St., N.W. (Georgetown). Historic house museum of the

Old Stone House

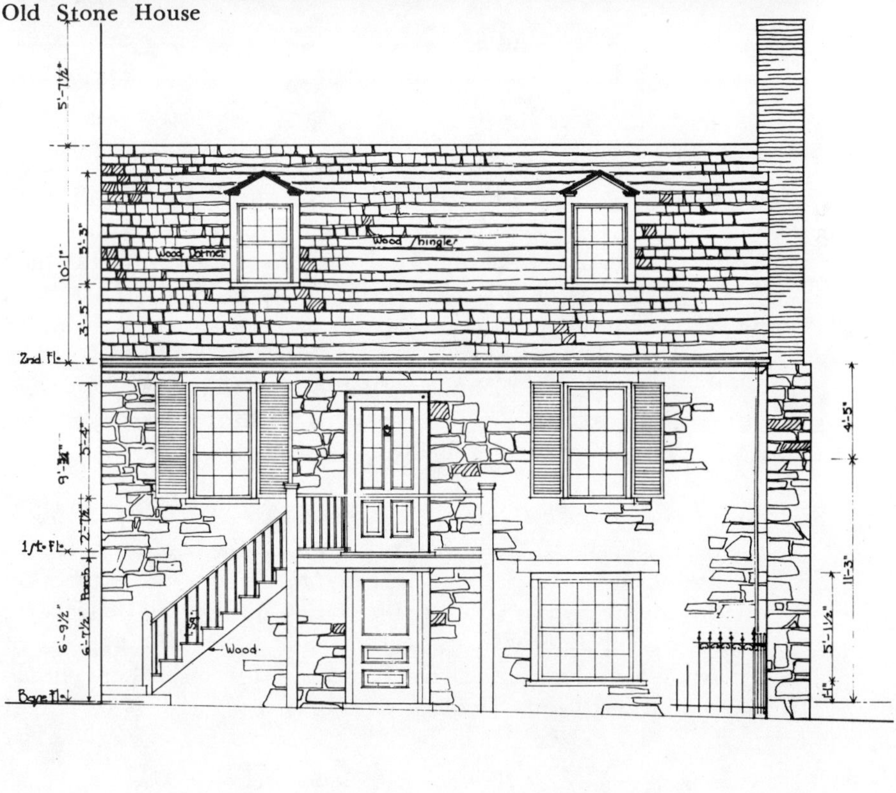

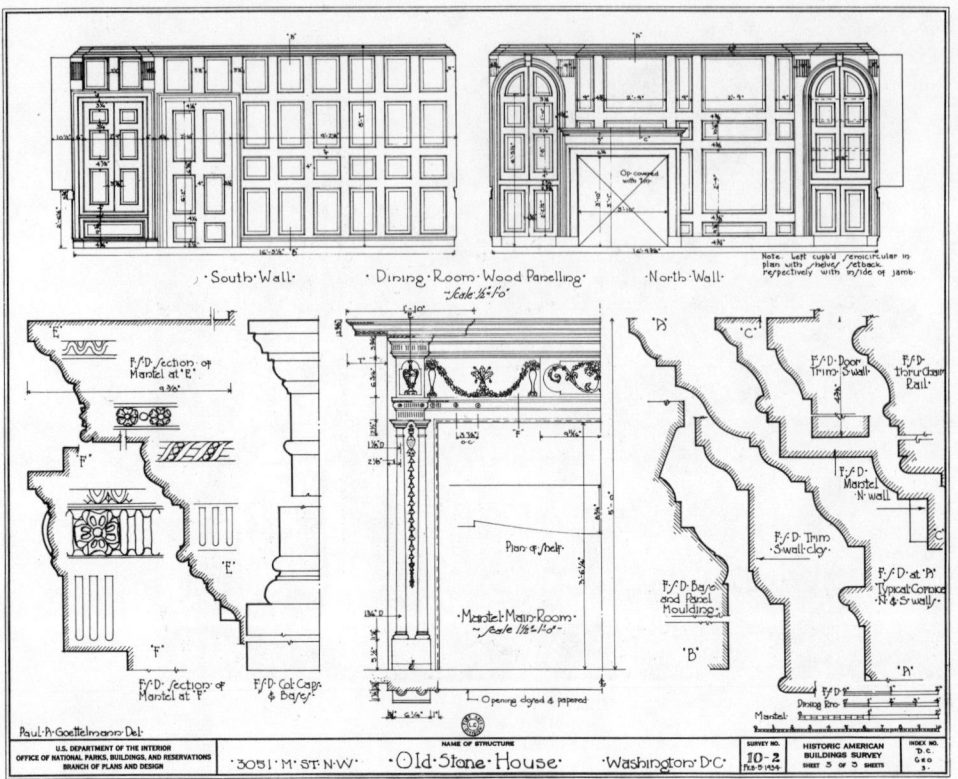

National Park Service. Rubble masonry, L-shaped, on sloping site, two-and-a-half stories on S. and E., principal entrance on second floor, N. room has fine paneling of later date. Front portion built c. 1765 probably by Christopher and Rachael Layhman, rear wing added by 1775 perhaps by Cassandra Chew; after 1800 ground floor used as shop; restored 1958-59 by the National Park Service. One of oldest buildings in the District of Columbia. 3 sheets (1934, including plans, elevations, section, details); 6 ext. photos (1935, 1971*), 1 int. photo (1935); 3 data pages (1936). NPS, JCL II

Owens, Isaac, House (Gannt-Williams House) (DC-62), 2806 N St., N.W. (Georgetown). Brick row house, 30′ (three-bay front) x 75′ (including later frame additions), two-and-a-half stories on raised basement, gable roof, semicircular fanlight with tracery, splayed stone lintels with keystones, side hall plan. Typical of Georgetown's Federal style row houses. Built 1816-17; renovation and rear additions 1921. 1 ext. photo (1942). NR, JCL II

Patent Office Building

Pakistani Chancery. See Francis B. Moran House (DC-268), 2315 Massachusetts Ave., N.W. at intersection with Decatur Pl.

Parrott, Thomas, House. See Teresa Fenwick House (DC-83), 3512 P St., N.W. (Georgetown).

Patent Office Building (later U.S. Civil Service Commission, now National Portrait Gallery and National Collection of Fine Arts) (DC-130), bounded by 7th, 9th, F, and G Sts., N.W. S. wing sandstone with granite ground floor, E., W., and N. wings marble, 402'-8" (thirty-one-bay front) x 274'-3" (twenty-one bays), built around an open central court, three stories, rusticated ground floor serves as podium for two-story Doric pilasters with full entablature, each facade has central Doric pedimented portico, that on S. facade is octastyle dipteral patterned after the Parthenon, principal interior features are curving double stairway in S. wing, granite gallery, sandstone gallery, Lincoln Gallery, and the remodeled Library and model

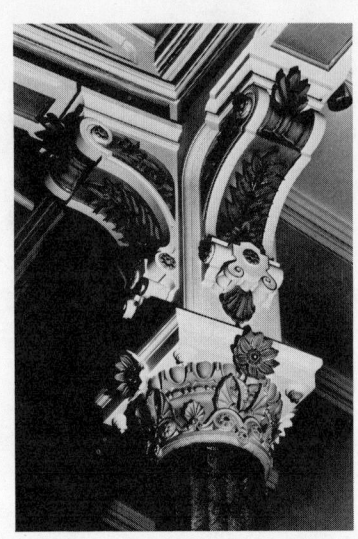

Patent Office Building

hall, vaulted brick fireproof construction. A foremost example of Greek Revival architecture in the U.S. S. wing built 1836-40; probably designed by William P. Elliot, construction supervised by Robert Mills; E. wing built 1849-52, W. wing 1856-62, N. wing completed 1867; supervisors of construction for E., W., and N. wings were Mills, Thomas U. Walter, and Edward Clark. 1877 fire destroyed upper floor of S., W., and N. wings; restored in flamboyant "Modern Renaissance" style by Cluss and Schulze, architects; restored for museum use 1964-67; Faulkner, Fryer, and Faulkner and Bayard Underwood, architects. Largest government office building in 19th C.; held numerous government agencies; Clara Barton and Walt Whitman employed there; scene of Lincoln's second Inaugural Ball. 9 ext. photos (1968*), 17 int. photos (1968*), 5 ext. photocopies (1859, c. 1889, 1891, 1907); HABSI form (1955). NHL, JCL I

Patterson, Edgar, House (DC-177), 1241 30th St., N.W. (Georgetown). Brick first floor, frame above, bracketed over-hang across front, 20' (three-bay front) x approx. 40' (including kitchen addition), two stories with basement exposed in rear, gable roof with ridge perpendicular to street, large central chimney, side hall plan. Built before 1811; three-story kitchen wing added in late 19th C. at NE. corner; house probably originally one-story with basement which was exposed when street grade was lowered c. 1830. 2 ext. photos (1968, 1969), photocopy of sketch plan (1968); 10 data pages (1968).

Patterson House (Washington Club) (DC-270), 15 Dupont
Circle, N.W. Marble facing with terra-cotta trim, irregular
A-shape, legs of A frame 27'-5" entrance facade with loggia
above, P St. and Dupont Circle elevations are 39', four stories,
truncated-hipped roof, modillion cornice with dentil course,
corner quoins, pedimented windows on second floor, elaborate
terra-cotta ornament of swags, drapes and garlands, varigated
marble panels between second and third floor windows,
elaborate interior wood and plaster trim. Built 1901-3; McKim,
Mead and White, architects; Stanford White, partner in charge;
two-story addition to E. 1956. Built for Robert W. Patterson,
editor of the *Chicago Tribune*, later home of his daughter
"Cissy" Patterson, owner of the Washington *Times-Herald*.
President and Mrs. Coolidge resided here in 1927 during White
House refurbishing. 3 ext. photos (1970*, 1971*, 1973*), 2 int.
photos (1971*), 2 photocopies of original drawings (1901*); 19
data pages (1970-73*). NR, JCL II

Patterson House

Peirce, Isaac, Mill (DC-22), NW. corner Tilden St. and Beach
Dr., N.W. (Rock Creek Park). Museum. Coursed granite rubble,
three-bay front, two-and-a-half stories sloping to three-and-a-
half stories on water side, gable roof, open plan, undershot

wheel; stone springhouse (1801), distillery (1811), and barn remain from Peirce Plantation. Built c. 1829 by Isaac Peirce; numerous changes to wheel and machinery; operated as grist mill until 1897; restored to operating condition by W.P.A. 1934-36. 19 ext. photos (1934, 1935, 1936 showing restoration, also views of millrace, barn, and springhouse), 3 photocopies (1899, c. 1900); 7 data pages (1936). NPS, JCL II

Peirce, Joshua, House. See Linnean Hill (DC-11), 3545 Williamsburg Lane, N.W.; Rock Creek Park near intersection of Klingle Rd. and Porter St., N.W.

Pension Building (DC-76), N. side of Judiciary Square, between 4th, 5th, G, and F Sts., N.W. Brick, 400' (twenty-seven bays) x 200' (thirteen bays), three stories with a fourth gallery story under the roof, sloping roofs over offices, large cross-gable clerestories provide light and ventilation for central court, design based on the Renaissance Farnese Palace, terra-cotta frieze depicting Union soldiers and sailors encircles building above first floor, interior organized around 316' x 116' courtyard 159' high, arcaded passages around court provide

Pension Building

Pension Building

access to offices, court divided into three sections by eight massive marbleized brick Corinthian columns, engineering innovations such as vertical clerestory windows and double pane windows to insulate against heat. Built 1882-85; Gen. Montgomery C. Meigs, architect; Caspar Buberl, sculptor of frieze. Housed agency which distributed pensions to Civil War veterans. Scene of several inaugural balls. 15 ext. photos (1959, 1967*, 1968*), 8 int. photos (1959, 1967*), 2 photocopies of drawings (1883*); 2 data pages (1959). NR, JCL I

Perry Building (DC-221), 821 Market Space (Pennsylvania Ave.) at 9th St., N.W. Brick and sheet metal, 50' (six-bay front) x 75 ' (eight bays), four stories, flat roof, segmental-arched windows, paneled frieze, modillion cornice. Original (western) portion probably built by 1860; eastern addition 1902-3; later alterations. 3 ext. photos (1967, 1969); 6 data pages (1969).

Peruvian Embassy. See Wilkins House (DC-276), 1700 Massachusetts Ave., N.W.

Peter, Robert, Houses (DC-70), 2618-20 K St., N.W. Brick row houses with later rough stucco covering, 2618 has three-bay front, 2620 has altered facade with three windows and a three-sided bay on each floor, three-and-a-half stories on raised basements, gable roofs, side hall plans, two-story rear ells covered by single gable roof, entrance of 2618 has straight transom and side lights. Two of five units built by Robert Peter for his sons c. 1795; altered; three units burned, remaining two demolished. Residents included Martha Parke Custis Peter, granddaughter of Martha Washington, and Anthony Merry, first British minister to live in Washington. 4 ext. photos (1959, details of facade only); 2 data pages (1959); HABSI form (1956).

Peter, Thomas, House. See Tudor Place (DC-171), 1644 31st St., N.W. (Georgetown).

Petersen House (House Where Lincoln Died) (DC-165), 516 10th St., N.W. Historic house museum of the National Park Service. Brick, three-bay front, three stories on raised basement, flat roof, modillion cornice, flat-arched windows, entrance has simple classical enframement and straight transom, side hall plan. Built 1849; a rear room added after 1878; purchased by government 1896; restored 1959. Typical Washington row house to which the dying President Lincoln was carried from Ford's Theater across the street. 2 ext. photos (1968*). NPS, JCL I

Philippine Embassy. See Emma S. Fitzhugh House (DC-260), 2253 R St., N.W.

Pierce, Isaac, House (DC-14), 711 6th St., S.E. Frame with clapboarding, 48′-7″ (front) x 32′-5″, two-story central section with gable roof flanked by one-story projecting wings with shed roofs, wings have false fronts, porch enclosed by wings has two Tuscan columns and balustraded deck, brick basement exposed in rear. Built c. 1830; demolished. 6 sheets (1936, including plans, elevations, details); 2 ext. photos (1936), 1 int. photo (1936).

Potomac Aqueduct (DC-166), Georgetown Abutment at N. bank of Potomac River, adjacent to extension of 36th St., N.W. (Georgetown), south abutment W. of junction of Key Bridge and the Virginia Shore. Originally wooden superstructure on stone piers driven to bedrock, c. ¼-mile long, carried C & O Canal across Potomac River. Built 1833-43; Major William Turnbull, engineer. Altered to two decks for canal and toll road, 1868; superstructure changed to iron 1888; superstructure removed 1933; most of piers destroyed 1962. 4 sheets (1970*, including plan, elevations, details of remaining arches); 9 photos (1967), 8 photocopies (c. 1860, c. 1865, c. 1868-87, 1879-87, 1900, c. 1910, c. 1924, c. 1940), 5 photocopies of original drawings (c. 1841); 17 data pages (1967).

Potomac Aqueduct, c. 1865 view

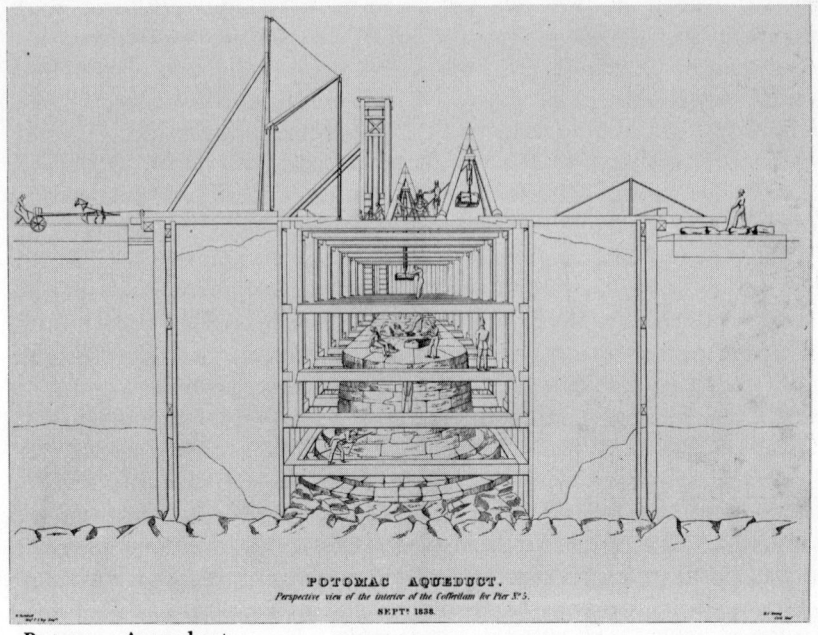

POTOMAC AQUEDUCT.
Perspective view of the interior of the Cofferdam for Pier Nº 5.
SEPTr 1838.

Potomac Aqueduct

Potomac Lodge No. 5 (now Doxiadis Associates) (DC-153), 1058 Thomas Jefferson St., N.W. (Georgetown). Brick, 21'-7" (two-bay front) x 42'-8" (three bays), two stories, gable roof with false parapet on E. Built c. 1810; altered; renovated in 1962 when building on W. was joined to it. Earliest Masonic lodge building still standing in the city. Potomac Lodge chartered in 1806; continued to use building until 1840. 1 ext. photo (1974*); 19 data pages (1967*). JCL III

Potomac Savings Bank (now National Bank of Washington, Georgetown Branch) (DC-323), 1200 Wisconsin Ave., N.W. (Georgetown). Brick, 60' (nine-bay front) x 50', three stories, first floor sheathed in rusticated sandstone, entrance flanked by Doric columns supporting frieze and pediment, bracketed pressed metal cornice. Originally three buildings erected c. 1850; burned 1909; remodeled in present form as one building 1910. 1 ext. photo (1969); 2 data pages (1969).

Powhatan Hotel (Roger Smith Hotel) (DC-354), NE. corner Pennsylvania Ave. and 18th St., N.W. Brick with stone trim, trapizoidal shape, ten bays (W. front) x four bays, ten stories,

flat roof with modillion cornice, large first floor windows with
splayed voussoir motif in brick, side bays have double windows
above first floor, front bays have three windows (two very
narrow), two-story pilasters flank bays of ninth and tenth floors,
decorative cornices above first, seventh, and eighth floors, first
floor contains lobby, main dining room and cafe, originally
there were 300 guest rooms. Built 1911; Milburn, Heister & Co.,
architects; became Roger Smith Hotel in 1938; demolished 1975.
Roof garden was popular dining and dancing spot for many years.
Washington Monument first illuminated in 1925 by spotlight on
hotel roof; illuminations continued during tourist season until
1931. 4 ext. photos (1974*, 1975*), 2 int. photos (1974*).

Prospect House (Gen. James Lingan House) (DC-210), 3508
Prospect St., N.W. (Georgetown). Brick, approx. 35' (three-bay
front) x 40', rear wing 25' x 50', west service wing 30' x 25',
two-and-a-half stories on raised rubble basement, gable roof,
raking parapets, end chimneys, pedimented dormers with
tracery, recessed round-arched entrance, tracery in fanlight,
pedimented architrave, side hall plan. Built between 1788 and
1793, probably for James Lingan, Revolutionary War general;
renovated and service wing added 1934; James W. Adams,
architect; renovated again c. 1951. Home of a number of
prominent persons including James E. Forrestal, first secretary
of defense. Served as official government guest house 1949-51.
1 ext. photo (1968*); 29 data pages (1967*). NR, JCL II

Pullman House (Russian Embassy) (DC-270), 1119-25 16th St.,
N.W. Brick and stone, three-bay front, three-and-a-half stories,
steep slate mansard with segmentally-arched dormers, balustrade at eaves, rusticated ground floor, second story windows
with triangular pediments, decorative tympanums, third story
windows with small iron balconies, Louis XV transitional style,
ornate interiors, grand stair with wrought-iron railing. Built
1909-11; Wyeth and Sullivan, architects; chancery wing added
to S.; refurbished 1933; Eugene Schoen, architect. Built by wife
of sleeping car inventor; sold to Russians 1913; remained vacant
from 1920 until 1934, when U.S. recognized Soviet government; reopened 1934. 1 ext. photo (1970*). JCL III

Quality Hill. See John Thomson Mason House (DC-167), 3425
Prospect St., N.W. (Georgetown).

Ray, Alexander, House (now F Street Club) (DC-44), 1925 F
St., N.W. Brick, five-bay front, two-and-a-half stories on raised

basement, low gable roof, attic windows in frieze, denticulated cornice with egg-and-dart and meander moldings, pediment on consoles above entrance a later addition, side oriel, rear ell. Built c. 1853; children's playroom (now dining room) added by Charles Norton, secretary to President Taft; house renovated 1924 by Laura Curtis; since 1933 house has served as exclusive private club under the direction of Mrs. Curtis (now Mrs. Gross), noted for its distinguished membership. 3 ext. photos (1936, 1974*). A house (DC-131) with similar details was on I St. between 18th and 19th Sts., N.W. JCL II

Ray's Warehouse and Office (now Corson and Gruman Company) (DC-148), 3260-62 K St., N.W. (Georgetown). Adjoining brick buildings, irregular L-shape, 89' x 64', 3260 has mono-pitch roof, 3262 has gable roof; 3262 built as warehouse c. 1855; 3260 built as office c. 1885; demolished. Earlier structure is one of original dock buildings of important Georgetown milling firm, A. Ross Ray & Bro. 3 ext. photos (1967), 1 int. photo (1967), photocopy of sketch plan (1967); 13 data pages (1967).

Reckert House (DC-120), 3232 M St., N.W. (Georgetown). Frame with clapboarding, approx. 30' (three-bay front) x 65' (including addition), two-and-a-half stories, gable roof. Built late 18th C, probably as a residence; first floor shop front added 19th C.; extensively altered and refurbished 1963. 1 ext. photo (1966); 5 data pages (1966).

Red Cross (American National) (DC-347), SW. corner of 17th and E Sts., N.W. White Vermont marble, eleven bays (E. front) x five bays, three stories on raised basement, third story recessed behind balustrade, hipped roof with tall interior chimneys, projecting tetrastyle Corinthian entrance portico with pediment, remaining bays of principal facade are separated by two-story engaged Corinthian columns, end elevations have slightly projecting unpedimented porticoes, entrance lobby features curving marble stair, assembly room on N. side of second floor has three stained-glass windows by Tiffany Studios. Built 1915-16; Trowbridge and Livingston, architects; Boyle-Robertson Company, builders. Headquarters of the nation's largest official relief organization. Building erected with public and private funds and dedicated as a memorial to the nurses of the Civil War. 4 ext. photos (1974*), 3 int. photos (1974*). NHL, JCL III

Red Cross, Tiffany windows

Red Wood. See Oak Hill (DC-42), Connecticut Ave. near Cathedral Ave., N.W.

Regency Row. See Eynon Building (DC-124), 3407 M St., N.W. (Georgetown).

Reintzel, Anthony, Building (DC-122), 3258 M St., N.W. (Georgetown). Brick, 24' (three-bay front) x approx. 70' (including ell), three stories, flat roof, side hall plan. Built c. 1808-12 probably as two-and-a-half story, gable-roofed house; extensive remodeling c. 1870-80 when roof raised, shop front, tin hood molds, and cornice added; demolished 1967. 1 ext. photo (1966); 6 data pages (1966).

Republic of China Chancery. See Gibson Fahnestock House (DC-259), 2311 Massachusetts Ave., N.W.

Rhodes Tavern (DC-326), 601-3 15th St., N.W. and 1431 F St., N.W. Brick with 20th C. stucco, originally L-shaped, approx. 40' (three-bay front) x 76' (eight bays), three stories, hipped roof, stone lintels in splayed voussoir-and-keystone pattern, denticulated cornice. Built 1800-1801 as a tavern; first floor extensively altered, five northern bays demolished 1957. Earliest commercial building remaining in downtown Washington; headquarters for British officers directing the burning of the White House; home of one of the first banks in the city and first home of firm which became Riggs National Bank. 1 ext. photo (1967*). NR, JCL II

Richards, Zalmon, House (DC-343), 1301 Corcoran St., N.W. First of a row of brick townhouses of unified design, two-bay front, two-and-a-half stories on raised basement, slate mansard roof, projecting wooden bays on front and side, scroll brackets at cornice of house and bays, cast-iron stair. Built c. 1880. Zalmon Richards was an important 19th C. educator, first president of National Teachers' Association which became National Education Association, instrumental in establishment of federal office of education, first superintendent of D.C. schools. 2 ext. photos (1974*). NHL, JCL III

Riggs National Bank, 17th and G Street Branch. See Washington Loan and Trust Company, West End Branch (DC-344), SW. corner 17th and G Sts., N.W.

Riggs National Bank, Washington Loan and Trust Branch. See Washington Loan and Trust Company (DC-217), SW. corner F and 9th Sts., N.W.

Riggs-Riley House (DC-46), 3038 N St., N.W. (Georgetown). Brick, 30' (three-bay front) x 42'-4" (not including rear ell), two-and-a-half stories, gable roof, round-arched entrance, molded surround with keystone and fanlight, flat-arched lintels with corner blocks, side hall plan, notable woodwork. Built 1813-16 by Romulus Riggs, a businessman; doctor's office added to E. by Dr. Joshua Riley, resident from 1826-75; service wing now replaces office. 12 sheets (1934*, including plans, elevations, details); 1 ext. photo (1974*); 1 data page (1941). JCL II

Rittenhouse Place. See Dumbarton House (DC-10), 2715 Q St., N.W. (Georgetown).

Robertson, Thomas, House (DC-115), 3116-18 M St., N.W. (Georgetown). Brick, 24' (four-bay front) x approx. 85' (including additions), three-and-a-half stories, gable roof, first

floor shop front, second and third floor windows have stone
lintels with splayed voussoir and keystones. Built c. 1812-13;
later additions and alterations. 1 ext. photo (1966); 6 data
pages (1966).

Roger Smith Hotel. See Powhatan Hotel (DC-354), NE. corner
Pennsylvania Ave. and 18th St., N.W.

Ross and Getty Building (DC-113), 3005-11 M St., N.W.
(Georgetown). Brick double building, each unit 27'-7" (three-
bay front) x 50', three-and-a-half stories, gable roof, solid stone
lintels of voussoir-and-keystone design, first floor doorways of
voussoir-and-keystone and fanlighted types, facade has seven
bays, central bay has false shuttered window abutting party
wall, shop fronts on first floor, change in brickwork at first
floor probably indicates lowering of street level in 1870s. Built
between 1810 and 1812; preservation of this and adjoining
building (Thomas Sim Lee House) in 1952 by Historic
Georgetown, Inc. spurred revitalization of commercial area of
Georgetown. 3 ext. photos (1966, 1971*), 3 int. photos (1966);
7 data pages (1966). Also see drawing of E. half of building
filed under Thomas Sim Lee House (DC-65). JCL II

Ross, Andrew, Tenant House I (DC-174), 1208 30th St., N.W.
(Georgetown). Brick, L-shaped, 21'-6" (four-bay front) x 35',
three stories, gable roof, forms a pair with house to north,
separated from it by one-story passage with arched brick
entrance. Built 1810-11 by Andrew Ross, one of five buildings
he erected at corner of 30th and M Sts. (also see DC-113 and
DC-175 below); interior alterations. 2 int. photos (1968, for
ext. photo see Andrew Ross Tenant House II, DC-175),
photocopy of sketch plan (1968); 12 data pages (1968).

Ross, Andrew, Tenant House II (DC-175), 1210 30th St., N.W.
(Georgetown). Brick, L-shaped, 18'-6" (three-bay front) x 42'
including rear kitchen addition, three stories, gable roof, forms
a pair with house to south (DC-174), side hall plan, built with
shop on first floor, residence above, carved Federal style
mantels. Built 1810-11; restored 1967, Carroll Curtice, architect. 1 ext. photo (1969), 3 int. photos (1968), photocopy of
sketch plan (1968); 11 data pages (1968).

Row House (DC-327), 1901 F St., N.W. Brick, four-bay front,
two-and-a-half stories on raised basement, low hipped roof with
wide eaves, frieze windows flanked by paired brackets, recessed

Andrew Ross Tenant House II

entry capped by segmental pediment on consoles, segmental-arched windows, projecting bay on E., entrance hall has round end, curving stairway, simple heavy window and door moldings with curving corners. Probably built 1850s; altered; demolished 1970. 3 ext. photos (1969*), 9 int. photos (1969*).

Row Houses (DC-328), 1903-11 F St., N.W. Five brick row houses, three stories on raised basements, flat roofs, mid to late 19th C., three have projecting bays, various window and cornice treatments; demolished 1970. 9 ext. photos (1969*, including one view of entire block, two of 1903, one each of 1905, 1907 and 1909, three of 1911).

Row Houses (DC-53), 613-31 G St., S.W. Ten frame row houses with clapboarding, designed as a group, each house has three-bay front and two stories, side hall plans, two units on each end have cross-gable centered over party wall and gable roofs, third and fourth units from each end are slightly set back, central two units have dormered mansard roof, all units have bracketed cornices and one-story proches. Built c. 1870; demolished. 3 ext. photos (1958).

Row Houses (DC-345), 1700 Block of Q St., N.W. Originally a group of 62 three-story row houses extending along both sides of Q St. and around the corner onto 17th St., designed and built as a speculative venture by architect Thomas F. Schneider between 1889 and 1892. Houses on N. side have brownstone and greenstone facing, those on S. side are brick with stone trim, some have full turrets or oriel turrets, others have projecting bays and shaped gables, tiled mansard roofs, Richardsonian Romanesque details; seven houses at W. end of N. row are demolished. Represent popular taste of the late 19th C.; many of first owners were high military and government officials. 5 ext. photos (1972*). JCL III

Row Houses, 1700 Block of Q St., N.W.

Row Houses (DC-55), 601-13 6th St., S.W. Seven identical brick units, three-bay fronts, three stories, flat roofs, bracketed modillion cornice, entrances have arched architraves with heavy moldings, flat-arched windows. Probably built c. 1870; demolished. 2 ext. photos (1958).

Ruppert, Anton, House (DC-6), c. ¼ mile from Bladensburg Rd. at New York Ave., N.E. Frame with clapboarding, 68'-5" (including wing on E. side) x 40'-11", one-and-a-half stories in front, sloping to two stories in rear, gable roof, cross gable with bull's-eye window over front entrance, flat and gable roofs on eastern wing, one-story porch with ogee arches and built-in seat on N. (front) facade, porch with lean-to roof across entire S. facade, interior chimneys parallel to ridge, central hall plan; two brick icehouses, one octagonal, one round. Built c. 1800; demolished. Ruppert, a butcher, purchased house 1865. 4 sheets (1936, including plans, elevations, section, details); 5 ext. photos (1935, including 2 of icehouses), 2 int. photos (1935); 6 data pages (1937).

Russian Embassy. See Pullman House (DC-270), 1119-25 16th St., N.W.

Saint John's Church (Episcopal) (DC-19), NE. corner 16th and H Sts., N.W., N. side of Lafayette Square. Stuccoed brick, approx. 48' x 33', one story with balcony, cross-gable roof, raised attic with cupola at crossing, hexastyle Doric portico topped by three-stage tower, Roman cross plan, interior hemispherical dome at crossing. Built 1816; Benjamin H. Latrobe, architect; originally a Greek cross plan with circular gallery, original transepts remain on N. and S.; nave extended, portico and tower added 1820-22; chancel enlarged, stenciling and stained glass added 1836-69; chancel further extended 1881-1900; James Renwick, architect; chancel faced with marble 1919-20; McKim, Mead and White, architects; structural repairs 1950-51. Considered by Latrobe to be one of his best designs, embodying his ideals of classical forms modified for the needs of the Protestant Church. Attended by many presidents. 13 sheets (1962, including plot plan, plans, elevations, sections, details); 8 ext. photos (1938, 1962), 3 int. photos (1962), 3 ext. photocopies (1888, c. 1890), 2 int. photocopies (c. 1860, post 1883), 3 photocopies of original sketches (c. 1816, 1822), 6 photocopies of original plans (1816); 31 data pages (1937-39, 1961, 1962). NHL, JCL I

Saint John's Church, 1816 watercolor by Benjamin H. Latrobe

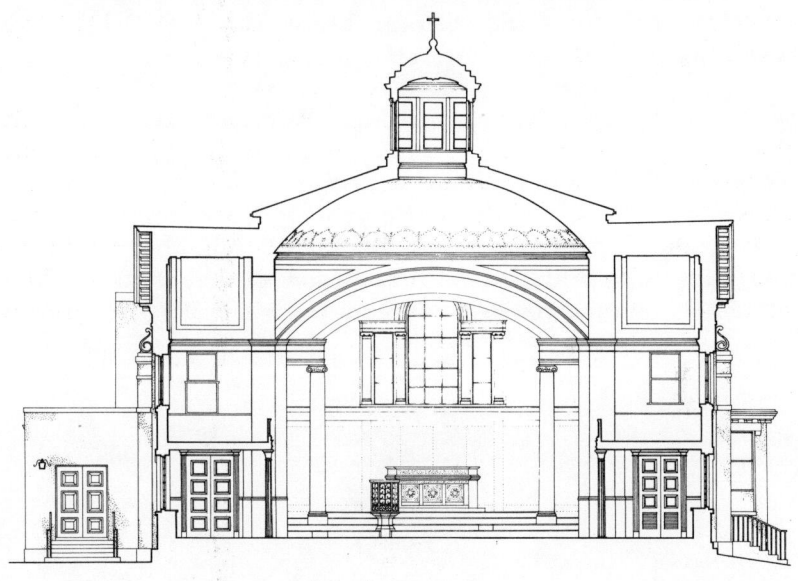

Saint Paul's Church (Episcopal) (DC-47), Rock Creek Cemetery, Rock Creek Church Rd., N.W., east of intersection of New Hampshire Ave. and Buchanan St., N.W. Brick, original portion 60′ x 48′-8″, one story, hipped roof, projecting 58′ high central entrance tower with octagonal louvered belfry, narrow round-arched windows, projecting chancel at rear. Built 1775 on site of 1719 church; remodeled 1868; burned 1921, original walls used in rebuilding by architect Delos Smith. Oldest church in District of Columbia; parish organized in 1712. 11 sheets (1953, including plan, elevations, interior elevations, details). NR, JCL II

Scottish Rite Temple, United Supreme Council, Prince Hall Affiliation, Southern Jurisdiction (DC-346), 1633 11th St., N.W. Brick, five-bay front, two stories, parapet, shallow hexastyle Ionic portico across front, Classical Revival details, eagle motif above entrances in end bays, sunburst in central bay. Probably built late 19th C.; first used as Scottish Rite meeting place c. 1907; portico a later addition; interiors remodeled c. 1948; demolished 1975. Prince Hall affiliation named for the man who organized the first Negro Scottish Rite lodge in Boston in 1772. 3 ext. photos (1974*).

Scott-Thropp House. See George Fraser House (DC-318), NE. corner R and 20th Sts., N.W. at Connecticut Ave.

Seven Buildings (DC-59), 1901-13 Pennsylvania Ave., N.W. Brick row houses, most with three-bay fronts, three and three-and-a-half stories, some with raised basements and areaways, gable roofs, arched doorways with coade stone keystones with women's heads in high relief; corner building five bays x five bays with rounded corner. Begun probably mid 1790s; altered for commercial use; numbers 1903 and 1913 demolished

Seven Buildings

19th C.; 1901, 1905, and 1907 demolished 1958; 1909 and 1911 remaining in altered form. 1901 served as executive mansion under Madison and housed the State Department. 5 ext. photos (1941, 1958 showing keystones); 1 data page (1958); HABSI form (1957).

Simms-Lihault House (DC-207), 3610 O St., N.W. (Georgetown). Brick, double house, approx. 32' (four-bay front) x 17' (not including rear additions), two stories, gable roof with raking parapets, end chimneys. Built probably between 1815 and 1818; extensive alterations and additions. 1 ext. photo (1968*); 21 data pages (1968*).

Sims House (DC-111), 2803 M St., N.W. (Georgetown). Brick, 34'-11" (four-bay front) x 95' (including additions), two-and-a-half stories on raised basement, gable roof, cantilevered balcony with cast-iron railing over areaway on S. Front. Built early 19th C.; rear additions and extensive alterations and renovation 1954. 1 ext. photo (1966); 5 data pages (1966).

Smith, Clement, House (Bodisco House) (DC-251), 3322 O St., N.W. (Georgetown). Brick, three-bay front, three-and-a-half stories on raised basement, gable roof, counter-sunk panels below windows, main entrance has elliptical fanlight and side lights, one-story pedimented entrance portico is supported by fluted columns and approached by curving double flight of stairs. Build 1815 by Georgetown builder Clement Smith; home of Alexander, Baron de Bodisco, Russian Ambassador 1838-54; divided into apartments; subsequently restored as single family dwelling. 3 ext. detail photos (1937, 1942, 1974*). JCL II

Smith-Morton Row House (DC-185), 3034 P St., N.W. (Georgetown). Brick, 22' (three-bay front) x 40', three stories, gable roof, fanlighted entrance in paneled recess, side hall plan, gabled brick outbuilding (original kitchen) shared with adjacent house. Built 1818-19. Well-preserved example of a modest Federal row house. 1 ext. photo (1969), 3 int. photos (1968), photocopy of sketch plan (1968); 12 data pages (1968).

Smith Row (DC-67), 3255-63 N St., N.W. (Georgetown). Five brick units, each three bays, three-and-a-half stories on raised basements, gable roofs, countersunk panels between floors, arched entrances with tracery. Built 1815 or 1816 by Clement and Walter Smith. One of the most handsome rows of Federal

Smith Row

style townhouses in Georgetown. 3 ext. photos (1942, 1974*). JCL II

Smithsonian Institution, Arts and Industries Building (DC-298), 900 Jefferson Dr., S.W. [50′ SE. of Smithsonian Institution Building (DC-141)]. Red brick with ornamentation of colored brick and sandstone, square, 325′ per side including projecting pavilions, exhibit spaces are one story of varying heights, pavilions containing offices are two-and-a-half stories, slate roofs with iron and steel frames exposed on interiors, symmetrical plan with four great exhibit corridors intersecting at central rotunda, corridors joined to corner pavilions by ranges, enclosed spaces form covered exhibition courts; rotunda is 108′ in height, corridors 56′ in height, both have lanterns and clerestory windows, in center of each facade are entrances flanked by two square towers, ample arched fenestration in walls for lighting exhibit spaces. Built 1879-81; Cluss and Schulze, architects;

design based on 1877 plan by Gen. Montgomery C. Meigs;
balconies and skylight added in exhibition areas 1897-1902.
Best remaining example of 19th C. "exposition" architecture in
U.S. Built to house international exhibits donated to U.S. after
Philadelphia Centennial Exhibition of 1876 and designed in the
manner of those buildings. 13 ext. photos (1975*); 6 data pages
(1971*). NHL, JCL II

Smithsonian Institution Building, photogrammetric drawing

Smithsonian Institution Building (DC-141), Jefferson Drive
between 9th and 12th Sts., S.W. Seneca sandstone, 447' x 160'
at widest point, five-part plan with central block, connecting
ranges and end wings of various heights, gable roofs; eight
towers with a variety of roof treatments and fenestration,
crenelated parapet, corbeled cornice, tall round-arched windows
with drip moldings, picturesque Norman style, W. wing with
apsidal end was originally library, E. wing contained living
quarters for secretary, central block had great exhibition hall
downstairs and lecture hall upstairs. Built 1847-55; James
Renwick, Jr., architect; upper floors of central block burned
1865, repairs and alterations by Adolf Cluss; E. wing and range
raised 1884; Cluss & Schulze, architects; numerous other
alterations before 1915; building renovated 1968-70; Chatelain,
Samperton, and Nolan, architects. First building of the Smithsonian Institution. A foremost example of medieval revivalism. 6
sheets (1963 including elevations, details); 13 ext. photos
(1968*, 1975*), 4 int. photos (1968*); 16 photogrammetric
stereopairs (1963*); 14 data pages (1971*). NHL, JCL I

Smithsonian Institution, Renwick Gallery. See Corcoran Gallery of Art (DC-49), NE. corner Pennsylvania Ave. and 17th St., N.W.

Society of the Cincinnati Headquarters. See Larz Anderson House (DC-255), 2118 Massachusetts Ave., N.W.

Southeast Neighborhood Area Study: Canal, Carroll, and Potomac Sts., S.E., (DC-71).

Row Houses, Canal St. at Independence Ave. Brick, two-bay fronts, two stories, flat roofs, corbeled brick cornices (a few with wooden cornices), bracketed cornice on consoles over entrance. Built late 19th C.; demolished 1960s. 5 ext. photos (1959).

House, 101 Carroll St. Brick with Greek Revival doorway. Demolished 1960s. 1 ext. photo (1959, doorway).

Row Houses, 122-24 Carroll St. Frame, two-bay fronts, two stories on raised basement, low gable roof. Built mid 19th C.; altered; demolished 1960s. 2 ext. photos (1959).

House, 1008 Potomac St. Brick, three-bay front, two-and-a-half stories, gable roof, side hall plan, rear ell. Built early 19th C.; later one-story wooden porch; demolished 1960s. 1 ext. photo (1959).

Double House, 1014 Potomac St. Stuccoed brick, four-bay front, two stories, flat roof, molded wooden cornice, later one-story porch. Probably built mid 19th C.; demolished 1960s. 1 ext. photo (1959).

Double House, 1016-18 Potomac St. Stucco, probably on brick, three-bay front, two stories, gable roof, central chimney, side hall plans, later porches. Built early 19th C.; demolished 1960s. 1 ext. photo (1959).

Southeast Neighborhood Area Study: North Carolina and Virginia Aves., S.E., (DC-72).

Double House, 156-58 North Carolina Ave. Brick, each unit two bays, three stories, gable roof, large central chimney. Built early 19th C.; altered; restored. 1 ext. photo (1959).

Row Houses, 306-8 Virginia Ave. Brick with stone trim, three-bay fronts, two-and-a-half stories, gable roofs, 306 has semicircular-arched doorway and flat splayed window lintels

with keystones, 308 has flat-arched windows and door with
corner drops. Built early 19th C.; demolished 1960s. 1 ext.
photo (1959).

House, 330 Virginia Ave. Brick, entrance in truncated corner,
three-and-a-half stories, intersecting gable roofs, unusual
arched treatment of triple windows on two principal facades.
Built early 19th C.; demolished 1960s. 3 ext. photos (1959).

May-Smallwood House, 324-26 Virginia Ave. Brick with stone
trim, eight-bay front, two-and-a-half stories on full raised
basement, gable roof, belt course, splayed lintels with
keystones, semicircular entrance architrave with keystone.
Built c. 1800 by Frederick May; later home of D.C. mayor
Samuel Smallwood; demolished 1960s. 3 ext. photos (1959).

Row Houses, 706-8 Virginia Ave. Stuccoed brick, three-bay
fronts, two-and-a-half stories on raised basement, gable roofs.
Built early 19th C.; later cast-iron steps; demolished 1960s. 1
ext. photo (1959).

Naval Lodge No. 4 Masonic Hall, NW. corner 5th St. and
Virginia Ave. Brick, three-bay front, six-bay flank, three
stories on raised basement, front and rear parapets, corner
pilasters, lancet-arched windows, corbeled cornice. Built c.
1821 as two story building; raised to three stories c. 1867;
after Naval Lodge moved to new hall at 4th and Pennsylvania
Ave., S.E. in 1895, building became meeting place for several
Negro Masonic organizations; demolished 1960s. 4 ext.
photos (1959).

Southeast Neighborhood Area Study: G, I, K, and L Sts., S.E.
(DC-73).

House, 600-2 G St. Brick, five-bay front, three stories, gable
roof, doorway has straight transom and side lights, triple
window above. Built early 19th C.; probably originally one
unit; rear addition with brick hood molds and corbeled
cornice. 2 ext. photos (1959).

House, 1101 G St. Stucco, probably over brick, three-bay
front, two stories, gable roof, denticulated cornice, side hall
plan. Built early 19th C.; altered. 1 ext. photo (1959).

House, 1002 I St. Brick, three-bay front, three stories on
slightly raised basement, flat roof, modillion and bracketed
cornice, entrance has supporting consoles. Built mid 19th C.;
demolished 1960s. 1 ext. photo(1959).

House, 1006 I St. Brick, three-bay front, three stories on slightly raised basement, flat roof, splayed lintels with keystones, simple pilastered door enframement, applied cornice, cast-iron stairs. Built early 19th C.; probably raised one story in mid 19th C.; demolished 1960s. 1 ext. photo (1959).

Houses, 808-10 K St. 808 is stuccoed, two-bays, two stories, flat roof, modillion cornice, probably built mid 19th C.; 810 is frame with narrow decorative siding laid horizontally, vertically, and diagonally, two-bays, one projecting, three stories, flat roof, built late 19th C. Both demolished 1960s. 1 ext. photo (1959).

Row Houses, 812-14 K St. Brick, each has two bays, two stories, flat roof, corbeled cornice, brick hood molds. Built late 19th C.; demolished 1960s. 1 ext. photo (1959).

House, 1016 K St. Brick, three-bay front, two-and-a-half stories, gable roof, central chimney. Built early 19th C.; demolished 1960s. 2 ext. photos (1959).

Double House, 817-19 L St. Brick, two-bay fronts, two stories, gable roof, central chimney. Built early 19th C.; altered. 1 ext. photo (1959).

Southeast Neighborhood Study: 1st, 2d, 6th, 7th, 9th, 10th, and 11th Sts., S.E. (DC-74).

Capitol Hill Club 214 1st St. Brick, three-bay front, two stories on raised basement, gable roof, rear ell, simple classical entrance architrave, brick dentils, cast-iron window grilles. Built early 19th C.; once the home of Peggy O'Neale; demolished 1960s. 1 ext. photo (1959).

House, 215 2d St. Frame with clapboarding, four-bay front, two stories, flat roof, modillion cornice and window cornices, spindlework porch. Built mid 19th C.; demolished 1960s. 1 ext. photo (1959).

House, 219 2d St. Brick, three-bay front, two stories on raised basement, wooden lintels with corner blocks, one-story wooden entrance porch. Built early 19th C.; demolished 1960s. 1 ext. photo (1959).

Watterston, George, House, 224 2d St. Brick, three-bay front with side addition, three stories on fully raised basement, flat roof, cornice with garland decoration, lintels with corner blocks, cast-iron gallery. Built sometime between 1802 and

Southeast Neighborhood Study,
House, 1016 K St.

1819, probably by George Watterston who was librarian of Congress, clerk of the House of Representatives, and founder and first secretary of the Washington Monument Society. 1 ext. photo (1959). JCL II

House, 235 2d St. Brick, three-bay front, two-and-a-half stories on raised basement, gable roof, sawtooth cornice, flat lintels with corner blocks, straight transom with tracery, curving iron stairs. Built early 19th C.; demolished 1960s. 1 ext. photo (1959).

Row Houses, 316-26 2d St. Brick, all have three-bay fronts, two and two-and-a-half and three stories, flat and mansard-fronted roofs, modillion cornices, decorative window hoods. Built late 19th C. 3 ext. photos (1959).

House, SE. corner 6th and G Sts. Brick, five-bay front, two stories plus a story in concave mansard roof, door frame has elaborate consoles. Built mid 19th C.; later rear addition. 2 ext. photos (1959).

B. B. French School, NW. corner 7th and G Sts. Brick with stone trim, six irregular bays (front) x four bays, two stories on raised basement, low mansard roof, first floor has flat lintels, second floor has semicircular arches, Tuscan entrance portico. 2 ext. photos (1959).

Row Houses, 1103-5 9th St. Brick, two-bay front, two stories, gable roofs, common chimney and areaway. Built early 19th C. 1 ext. photo (1959).

House, SE. corner 10th and K Sts. Brick, three-bay front, two-and-a-half stories, gable roof, flat lintels with corner blocks. Built early 19th C.; demolished 1960s. 2 ext. photos (1959).

Philadelphia Row, 132-44 11th St. Brick row, each unit three bays on first floor, two above, three stories, flat roofs, bracketed cornices, semicircular-arched doors, side hall plans, some have interior plasterwork remaining. Built 1865-66 by Charles Gessford. 4 ext. photos (1959). JCL III

House, 900 11th St. Frame with clapboarding, five-bay front, two stories on raised basement, gable roof, central hall plan, rear additions, cast-iron stairs. Built mid 19th C.; demolished 1960s. 2 ext. photos (1959).

Row Houses, 903-5 11th St. Frame, two-bay fronts, two stories on raised basement, gable roof, common chimney, now covered with artificial brick siding. Built early 19th C. 1 ext. photo (1959).

Stanley, Arthur C., House (DC-271), 2370 Massachusetts Ave., N.W. Brick with stone trim, 55′ (four-bay facade) x 41′, 38′-6″ x 25′ service wing, three stories, slate gable roof with shaped and stepped ends, slightly projecting end pavilion with shaped gable, small-paned casement windows, Jacobean country house style, Jacobean and early Georgian interior details. Built 1930; Smith and Edwards, architects. 2 ext. photos (1970*, 1971*), 4 int. photos (1973*); 2 data pages (1970-73*).

State, War, and Navy Building (now Old Executive Office Building) (DC-290), SE. corner Pennsylvania Ave. and 17th St., N.W. Granite, rectangular with two inner courtyards, approx. 285′ (twenty-five-bay Pennsylvania Ave. facade) x 520′ (forty-five bays), complex slate mansard roof with decorative chimneys and dormers, each facade had projecting central pavilion of seven stories, remainder of building is six stories (including basement and two stories under mansard), subbasement under entire building, central pavilions and slightly projecting corner pavilions ornamented with grouped columns and pilasters, pedimented windows; interior originally divided between State, War, and Navy departments with distinctive hardware for each department, six spiral stairways (two of them double) with domed skylights, three highly ornamented departmental libraries, over ten acres of floor space. Built wing by wing, begun 1871, completed 1888; designed by Alfred B. Mullett, supervising architect of the Treasury; completion supervised by Col. Thomas L. Casey; designer Richard von Ezdorf responsible for much of interior decoration and exterior sculpture. A premier example of the French Second Empire style, more popularly known as the "General Grant" style. 10 ext. photos (1969*). NHL, JCL I

Stewart, Alexander, House (Embassy of Luxembourg) (DC-272), 2200 Massachusetts Ave., N.W. Brick with limestone facing, irregular five-sided plan, 72'-6" (principal five-bay Massachusetts Ave. facade) x 31'-4" (two-bay 22d St. facade) x 93'-2" (five-bay Q St. facade), three-and-a-half stories, slate mansard roof, balustrade at eaves, rusticated first floor, projecting entrance vestibule, smooth panels flank recessed second and third story windows, second floor windows round-arched with scroll keystones, decorative spandrels, Louis XV style, elaborate interiors with Jacobean and Georgian Revival features. Built 1908-9; J. H. de Sibour, architect. Built for Alexander Stewart, congressman from Wisconsin; became Luxembourg Legation 1941. 2 ext. photos (1970*), 5 int. photos (1970*), photocopy of original drawing (1908*), photocopy of plan (1972*); 13 data pages (1970-73*).

Stoddert, Benjamin, House. See Halcyon House (DC-69), 3400 Prospect St., N.W. (Georgetown).

Stohlman's Confectionary (DC-104), 1254 Wisconsin Ave., N.W. (Georgetown). Brick, 29'-7" (slightly irregular four-bay front) x 97'-2", three stories, molded brick cornice, segmental pediment of pressed metal, flat roof. Built c. 1880s; first floor ice cream parlor interior removed to Smithsonian Institution, Museum of History and Technology 1957; interiors extensively altered. 2 ext. photos (1966), 3 int. photos (1966, including one view of Smithsonian installation); 5 data pages (1966).

Sulgrave Club. See Herbert Wadsworth House (DC-274), 1801 Massachusetts Ave., N.W.

Sullivan, Jeremiah, Building (DC-202), 1331 35th St., N.W. (Georgetown). Brick commercial building, 18' x 40', two

Stohlman's Confectionary, Smithsonian Installation

stories, low pitched roof, pressed metal oriel window at second floor, brick cornice, antefixæ and shaped parapet of pressed metal. Built 1891; top floor converted to residential use, first floor commercial; being remodeled for apartments 1974. 1 ext. photo (1968*); 13 data pages (1969*).

Tayloe, Benjamin Ogle, House (Cameron House) (DC-51), 25 Madison Pl., N.W. Brick, originally three-bay front, three-and-a-half stories, gable roof, entrance flanked by colonettes, hanging cast-iron balcony across second floor. Built 1823 by Benjamin O. Tayloe; entrance bay to N. with semicircular bow and Palladian window a later addition; purchased by Cosmos Club 1904; renovated 1967-68 as part of Lafayette Square redevelopment project. Home of Sen. James D. Cameron of Pennsylvania and Vice President Garrett A. Hobart. Known as "Little White House" when Mark Hanna held his political breakfasts there. 1 ext. photo (1958); 1 data page (1959); HABSI form (1957). JCL II

Tayloe, Col. John, House. See The Octagon (DC-25), 1799 New York Ave., N.W.

Tayloe, Col. John, House, Stable. See The Octagon Stable (DC-336), rear of 1799 New York Ave., N.W.

Temperance Fountain(DC-240), NE. corner Pennsylvania Ave. and 7th St., N.W. Granite, about 7' square, four Tuscan columns on pedestals, two-part entablature, pyramidal roof surmounted by bronze heron, cylindrical pedestal supporting pair of bronze dolphins. Erected 1882; presented by Henry D. Cogswell, a San Francisco dentist. 1 ext. photo (1967); 1 data page (1969).

Tiber Island Center for Cultural and Community Activities. See Thomas Law House (DC-20), 1252 6th St., S.W.

Tingey, Thomas, House. See Washington Navy Yard Commandant's House (DC-12), E. of main gate of Washington Navy Yard at 8th and M Sts., S.E.

Townsend House (Cosmos Club) (DC-273), 2121 Massachusetts Ave., N.W. Limestone facing, central three-and-a-half story block (three bays) with flanking two-story wings, 125'-1" x 123'-9", slate mansard roof on central block, truncated-hipped roofs on wings, segmental-arched dormers, balustrade at eaves, rusticated first floor, glass and metal marquise, central pavilion has four two-story fluted composite pilasters, design based on Petit Trianon at Versailles, interior designed for lavish entertaining with elaborate plasterwork, paneling, and marble trim. Built 1899-1901; Carrère and Hastings, architects (previous house on site, the Hillyer Mansion, incorporated into new structure); addition to N. 1904, Carrère and Hastings, architects; interiors altered, extensive modifications in 1950 after purchase by Cosmos Club; Horace Peaslee, architect; five-story addition to N. 1952. Built for Richard H. Townsend, retired president of Erie and Pittsburgh Railroad. 2 ext. photos (1970*, 1971*), 1 int. photo (1971*), 1 ext. photocopy (1950*), photocopy of house previously on site (prior to 1898*), 4 copies of preliminary plans (n.d.*), photocopy of site plan (1950*), photocopy of plan (1972*); 32 data pages (1970-73*). NR, JCL II

Tuckerman, Lucius, House (DC-78), 1600 I St., N.W. Brick with trim and basement of sandstone, three stories on raised basement, hipped roof, central pavilion, truncated corner and rear bay are sandstone faced, wall dormers, ornamental chimneys, asymmetrical fenestration, glass and metal marquise,

Richardsonian Romanesque style, classical detailing on interior. Built 1886; Hornblower and Marshall, architects; demolished 1967. 4 ext. photos (1959, 1967*), 3 int. photos (1967*); 2 data pages (1959).

Tudor Place (Thomas Peter House) (DC-171), 1644 31st St., N.W. (Georgetown). Brick with buff-colored stucco, five-part mansion plan, two-story central block with three-bay facades and hipped roof, one-story loggialike hyphens with balustraded eaves, two-story two-bay end blocks with hipped roofs, on S. facade a circular porch bisects the wall and is expressed on the exterior as a two-story Doric portico with semicircular dome, portico is flanked by triple windows set in recessed arches, N. facade is severely plain, notable interior woodwork and plaster-work. Two wings built c. 1794; wings remodeled and main house built c. 1805-16 for Thomas Peter and his wife Martha Custis, granddaughter of Martha Washington; William Thornton, architect. House has remained in family of builder until the present and is virtually unaltered. One of the unusual and innovative designs in American Federal domestic architecture. 22 ext. photos (1962*, 1967* including landscape details), 61 int. photos (1962*, 1967*). All photos are restricted and cannot be reproduced without permission. NHL, JCL I

Turkish Embassy. See Edward H. Everett House (DC-258), 1606 23d St., N.W. at Sheridan Circle.

Tyler, Grafton, Double House (DC-178), 1314 30th St., N.W. (Georgetown). Brick, facade of each unit has projecting three-sided bay and a one-bay entry, 22' (east front) x 75', two-and-a-half stories, slate mansard roof with eared segmental dormers on facade and sides, brick hood molds on windows, three tall paneled brick chimneys along each side, side hall plan, some original gas fixtures and mantels remain. Built 1868, rear kitchen portion altered 1960. 2 ext. photos (1968), 3 int. photos (1968), photocopy of sketch plan (1968); 13 data pages (1968).

Union of Burma Chancery. See Charles Evans Hughes House (DC-278), 2223 R St., N.W.

Union Station (DC-139), facing S. on Union Station Plaza at intersection of Massachusetts Ave., Louisiana Ave., and 1st St., N.E. Steel frame, Vermont granite facing, symmetrical plan of

Union Station

Roman Classical inspiration, facade 626' long, monumental central pavilion with three arched openings, engaged Ionic columns supporting allegorical figures, lower arcaded wings, end pavilions with arched carriage openings, principal waiting room is 120' x 219' with 96'-high barrel vaulted coffered ceiling, main concourse with access to platforms is 760' long, trimmed with white enamel brick and terra-cotta. Built 1903-8; Daniel H. Burnham, architect; Louis Saint-Gaudens, sculptor. Built as a monumental gateway to the capital; an important element of the McMillan Plan for Washington. To be remodeled for use as the National Visitors' Center. 17 ext. photos (1968*), 8 int. photos (1968*). NR., JCL I

U.S. Capitol (DC-38), at the intersection of North, East, and South Capitol Sts. and the Mall, forms the focal point for the city's street system; extensive grounds are bounded by Independence and Constitution Aves. and 1st St., S.E. and N.E., and 1st St., S.W. and N.W. Aquia sandstone and marble with cast-iron dome, two stories on rusticated podium, central and end porticoes, balustrade at eaves. The country's most important civic structure. Set precedent for Classical Revival style

U.S. Capitol

c. 1861 view showing dome under construction

WEST ELEVATION

U.S. Capitol, Gatehouses

in the public buildings of the new capital. Design competition won by William Thornton; building begun 1793; N. wing completed and occupied by Senate 1800; construction continued under Benjamin H. Latrobe 1803-17 including rebuilding after fire set by British in War of 1812; original low-domed building completed by Charles Bulfinch 1819-29; House and Senate wings and cast-iron dome added by Thomas U. Walter 1851-65; western terrace added and grounds landscaped 1875-92; Frederick Law Olmsted, landscape architect; E. front extended 1959 under J. George Stewart, architect of the Capitol. 19 ext. photos (c. 1934-35, 1975*), 2 ext. photocopies (c. 1861); HABSI form for E. front (1955). NHL, JCL I

Gatehouses (DC-31), originally at western entrance to Capitol grounds; one now located NE. corner 17th St. and Constitution Ave., N.W., one at NW. corner 15th St. and Constitution Ave., N.W. Rusticated Aquia sandstone, 15' square, one room plan, flat roof, arched entrance, flanking Doric columns supporting entablature with guillouche frieze, parapet with rinceau panel. Built c. 1814; attributed to Charles Bulfinch, then architect of the Capitol; moved to present location 1880; repaired after flood damage 1940. 2 sheets (1940, including plan, elevations, details); 10 ext. photos (1937, 1938, 1939), 2 photocopies of drawings (1924*); 14 data pages (c.1939). NPS, JCL II

Gateposts (DC-35), originally on grounds of Capitol, moved to the Mall at 7th St. and Constitution Ave., 15th St. and

Constitution Ave., N.W., and Fort Totten Park. Rusticated sandstone pillar, 5' square, guillouche frieze, scroll cap with palmette decoration. Built c. 1814; attributed to Charles Bulfinch, then architect of the Capitol. 9 ext. photos (1937, (1938), 2 photocopies of drawings (1924*). See 14 data pages filed under U.S. Capitol Gatehouses (DC-31). NPS, JCL II

Plaza Light Standards (DC-77), surrounding Capitol Plaza, E. of Capitol. Bronze posts, stone piers. Built after 1875; converted from gas to electricity. Designed by Thomas Wisedell, architect, under supervision of Frederick Law Olmsted, landscape architect. 2 ext. photos (1959).

Shelter (DC-75), on Capitol grounds, NE. of Capitol. Metal hipped roof, wrought-iron supports, carved wooden bench, originally served as horsecar stop for Hedric Company. Built late 19th C. under supervision of Frederick Law Olmsted, landscape architect. 3 ext. photos (1959).

U.S. Civil Service Commission. See Patent Office (DC-130), bounded by 7th, 9th, F, and G Sts., N.W.

U.S. Court of Claims. See Corcoran Gallery of Art (DC-49), NE. corner Pennsylvania Ave. and 17th Sts., N.W.

U.S. Custom House and Post Office (now U.S. Post Office, Georgetown Station) (DC-138), 1221 31st St., N.W. (Georgetown). Granite ashlar, 61' (five-bay front) x 46', two stories on raised basement, low hipped roof, denticulated cornice, 10'- wide paved terrace to S. and W., simple Italian Renaissance design, cast-iron beams, columns, and trusses used in construction, originally post office on first floor and custom house on second. Built 1857-58; designed by Ammi B. Young, supervising architect of the Treasury; 20th C. additions to N. and rear; interior remodeled. A remnant of the days when Georgetown was a flourishing port of entry. 11 sheets (1970, including plans, elevations, section, details); 2 ext. photos (1937, 1968), 5 int. photos (1969), photocopy of ext. view (n.d.), photocopy of int. view (n.d.), 6 photocopies of original 1857 plans, elevations, and sections, 2 photocopies of 1939 plans; 22 data pages (1969). NR, JCL II

U.S. Department of the Treasury (DC-348), 1500 Pennsylvania Ave., N.W. Granite, rectangle enclosing two inner courts,

U.S. Department of the Treasury

260′(twenty-one bays) x 466′ (forty-bay 15th St. facade), three stories on raised basement, gable roof, balustraded eaves; E. and central wings built 1836-42; Robert Mills, architect; originally built of Aquia sandstone, principal feature is monumental colonnade of thirty Ionic columns along E. side, interior has barrel-vaulted corridors and groin-vaulted offices for fireproof construction; S. wing is granite and has central pedimented octastyle Ionic portico, portions of original painted ceiling decoration recently uncovered, built 1855-61; Ammi B. Young, architect; W. wing built 1862-64; Isaiah Rogers, architect; has central octastyle pedimented portico flanked by two columns *in*

U.S. Department of the Treasury

antis, end pavilions have pedimented distyle *in antis* faces like those which flank colonnade on E.; N. wing built 1867-69; A. B. Mullett, architect; similar to S. wing, contains elaborate marble banking room; sandstone of E. facade replaced with granite 1908; attic floor added 1910. This and Patent Office (DC-130) are among the foremost examples of Greek Revival civic architecture in the country. 12 ext. photos (1974*, 1975*), 10 int. photos (1974*). NHL, JCL I

U.S. General Post Office (now U.S. Tariff Commission Building) (DC-219), between 7th, 8th, E, and F Sts., N.W. Marble and granite, rectangular with court, 204′ (nineteen bays) x 280′ (nineteen bays), three stories above basement, rusticated first story, two-story Corinthian order of pilasters having columns at central and secondary pavilions, details adapted from various classical models; offices both side of corridor in three wings, large room in fourth, brick groined and segmental vaulting in original portion, arched brick flooring on iron joists in addition, notable helical stairs lighted by cupolas, plaster ornament adapting Greek and Roman motifs, cast-iron door frames, Greek Doric entrance and vestibule. Built 1839-44; Robert Mills, architect and supervisor of construction; major addition 1855-66; Thomas U. Walter, architect; Montgomery C. Meigs, superintendent of construction; later additions inside court and below grade. 9 ext. photos (1969), 16 int. photos (1969), 3 ext. photocopies (1851 engraving, 1859 woodcut, photo n.d.); 19 data pages (1969). NHL, JCL II

U.S. Marine Corps Commandant's House (DC-134), 801 G St., S.E., at N. end of Marine Corps Barracks parade ground. Brick, 42' (four-bay front) x 32', two-and-a-half stories on raised basement, mansard roof with large dormers, fanlighted entry,

U.S. General Post Office, 1851 engraving

splayed lintels with keystones, denticulated cornice, rear facade comprised of two curving bays with three windows each, one-story rear porch, low flanking wings, central hall with groin vault. Built 1801 on site selected by President Jefferson; attributed to George Hadfield, architect. House originally had three-bay front, central hall and hipped roof with cupola; facade extended 16' E. in 1840; flanking wings added; renovated and mansard roof added 1891; Hornblower and Marshall, architects; rear porch enclosed 1907; numerous other alterations. Has served as residence of every Marine Corps Commandant since 1806. 6 ext. photos (1965, 1974*). NR, JCL II

U.S. Navy and Munitions Buildings (DC-324), S. side of Constitution Ave. between 17th and 21st Sts., N.W. Reinforced concrete, each building has unified facade fronting on Constitution Ave., together facades measure 1,700', perpendicular to facades are long parallel wings joined by bridges, Navy Building has ten wings, Munitions Building has eight wings, each wing 60' wide and 560' long, facades are three stories, wings have slightly set back fourth story (a later addition), flat roofs, large window areas. Built 1918; demolished 1970. Last to be demolished of the temporary buildings erected on the Mall during World Wars I and II. 7 ext. photos (1970*), 3 int. photos (1970*).

U.S. Navy Bureau of Medicine and Surgery, Potomac Annex, Building No. 2. See Naval Observatory, Old (DC-341), entrance to grounds at 23d and E Sts., N.W.

U.S. Post Office Department (DC-135), S. side of Pennsylvania Ave. between 11th and 12th Sts., N.W. Granite wall-bearing structure, 200' x 305', eight floors plus basement, mezzanine and full ninth story attic, picturesque chateau roof, 315'-high clock tower centered in principal facade, lower floors are rusticated, central bays of each facade set back creating four large corner pavilions, turreted corners, arcuated fenestration, ornamental dormers, Richardsonian Romanesque style, interior offices organized around 99' x 184' x 157'-high skylighted court, marble wainscoting in corridors, open cage elevators, ground floor of the central court enclosed for office space. Built 1892-99; Willoughby J. Edbrooke, supervising architect of the Treasury. 1 ext. photo (1967*), 4 int. photos (1967*), 1 ext. photocopy (early 20th C.*), photocopy of int. court (c. 1908*), copy of drawing of tower (1895*). NR, JCL II

U.S. Post Office Department

U.S. Post Office, Georgetown Station. See U.S. Custom House and Post Office (DC-138), 1221 31st St., N.W. (Georgetown).

U.S. Soldiers Home (Old Soldiers Home) (DC-353), entrance at Rock Creek Church Rd. and Upshur St., N.W.; grounds consist of c. 300 acres bounded by Rock Creek Church Rd., Harewood Rd., North Capitol St., Irving St., and 5th St., N.W. Established by Congress in 1851 as a home for old and disabled soldiers. Funds were supplied by Gen. Winfield Scott out of the indemnity paid to him by Mexico City in the Mexican War. Has grown from 127 inmates in 1859 to over 2,700. Located on one of highest points of land in city. Parklike grounds and views over city made the home a destination for pleasure excursions in late 19th and early 20th C. Campus now includes administrative, dormitory, and recreation buildings; a large hospital complex lies to south. 17 ext. photos of various buildings (1975*, including gatehouses, quarters, and water tower.) NHL

Corn Rigs (Anderson Cottage). Brick (stuccoed 1897), two-and-a-half stories, asymmetrical plan, gable roof with cross gables, wooden veranda, decorative bargeboards. Built c. 1843; summer home of George Riggs, who sold his farm to the Soldiers Home; used as first dormitory; served as summer retreat for Presidents Buchanan, Lincoln, Hayes, and Arthur; Lincoln finished final draft of Emancipation Proclamation here; he also named the building Anderson House in honor of Gen. Robert Anderson, who was commanding Fort Sumter when it was fired on. 6 ext. photos (1975*). JCL II

Scott Building (now Sherman South Building). Vermont marble, originally two-and-a-half stories with mansard roof and central mansarded clock tower. Built 1852-57; Lt. Barton S. Alexander, architect; Gilbert Cameron, builder; in 1869 mansard converted to a third floor with hipped roof, crenelated parapet, brick corbeling and corner turrets, tower roof changed to open arcade with turreted corners; now attached by an annex to the Sherman North Building (completed 1891 with similar architectural details.) First major building constructed at the Home; housed residents and administrative offices. 16 ext. photos (1974*, 1975*), 17 int. photos (1974*). JCL II

Quarters 1 and *2*. Marble facing, five bay facades, gable roofs, projecting entrance pavilions with steep gables, decorative window hoods, one story wooden porches; Quarters 2 has an open vestibule on first level of entrance pavilion and slightly different fenestration. Both built 1852-54; Lt. Barton S. Alexander, architect. 6 ext. photos (1975*, three of each building).

Chapel. Red sandstone, gable roof, bell cot, side entrance, Gothic Revival style. Built 1870-71; interiors altered; used for both Protestant and Catholic services. 7 ext. photos (1975*).

Stanley Hall. Marble facing, gable roof, central window with tracery and steep gable above, entrance porch, Gothic Revival style. Built 1897-98 as an amusement hall containing 700-seat auditorium. 6 ext. photos (1975*).

Grant Building. Marble, three stories, projecting central block and slightly lower wings, arcaded entrance, crenelated

U.S. Supreme Court Building

parapet, Gothic and Classical Revival details. Built 1910-12; served as quarters and principal mess. 6 ext. photos (1975*).

United States Storage Company (DC-311), 418 10th St., N.W. Brick, two-bay front, eight stories, flat roof, parapet pierced by arches, quadruple windows on second through sixth floors, pilaster strips join to form large arches at seventh floor, two double doors on first floor with canopy above. Built 1909. 1 ext. photo (1967*).

U.S. Supreme Court Building (DC-356), NE. corner 1st and East Capitol Sts., N.E. Vermont marble facing, 385' (twenty-three bays) x 305', tall central navelike section with gable tile roof, massive Corinthian entrance portico with richly carved pediment, similar but less ornate portico at rear, lower symmetrical hipped-roof wings are one story with basement, wings enclose open courtyards, low relief pilasters divide bays, monumental stair leads to central portico, cheek blocks support large allegorical figures, open plaza in front of building, balustraded terraces at sides. Built 1935; Cass Gilbert, architect. One of the last of the large neoclassical federal buildings erected in the 1930s. 2 ext. photos (1975*). JCL I

U.S. Tariff Commission Building. See U.S. General Post Office (DC-219), between 7th, 8th, E, and F Streets, N.W.

Van Hook, John, House See Frederick Douglass House (DC-97), 1411 W St., S.E.

Van Ness Mausoleum (DC-169), originally in the Burnes family burial grounds, H St. between 9th and 10th Sts., N.W., moved to Oak Hill Cemetery, entrance at 3001 R St., N.W. (Georgetown). Brick and stone, circular Doric colonnade supporting full entablature and domed roof, urn finial, based on Temple of Vesta in Rome. Built 1833; George Hadfield, architect. 2 ext. photos (1937). JCL II

Vigilant Firehouse (DC-98), 1066 Wisconsin Ave., N.W. (Georgetown). Brick, 24' front, two stories, two vehicular doors (one now a window) on first floor, three windows above, gable roof with gable end to street, wooden belfry. Built 1844 for private firefighting company; converted to commercial use 1883; side and rear additions. 4 sheets (1964, including plot plan, plans, elevation); 2 ext. photos (1964), 2 int. photos (1964); 7 data pages (1964). NR, JCL II

Volta Bureau (Alexander Graham Bell Association for the Deaf) (DC-245), 1537 35th St., N.W. (Georgetown). Yellow brick with terra-cotta trim, 32' (three-bay front) x 66'-8", originally one story plus exposed basement, four-level library stack area at rear, sloping roof, balustraded parapet, two composite columns *in antis* on W. facade, terra-cotta Corinthian cornice, Classical Revival design; originally had large reading room in front and stack area in rear. Built 1893-94; Peabody and Stearns, architects; remodeled 1948-49; Russell O. Kluge, architect; changes included insertion of a third floor and alteration of the fenestration. Volta Bureau founded By Alexander Graham Bell as a center for information on the education of deaf children. 5 ext. photos (1969), copy of 1948 ext. photo, 2 copies of 1894 int. photos, 4 photocopies of original perspective, plan, elevation, and section (c. 1893); 14 data pages (1969). NHL, JCL III

Wadsworth, Herbert, House (Sulgrave Club) (DC-274), 1801 Massachusetts Ave., N.W. Brick with stone trim, triangular shape with two rounded corners, 136' (Massachusetts Ave. facade) x 125' (P St.) x 76' (18th St.), three stories, balustrade at eaves, rusticated first floor, Palladian window above Massachusetts Ave. entrance, cast-iron balconies on bow corners, eclectic interior with elaborate paneling and plasterwork, first floor ballroom. Built c. 1900; Frederick H. Brooke, architect; became Sulgrave Club 1932. 2 ext. photos (1970*), 6 int. photos (1970*), 1 ext. photocopy (1906*), photocopy of plan (1972*); 2 data pages (1970-73*). NR, JCL II

Walker, David, House (DC-9), 932 27th St., N.W. Brick with stone trim, 16'-6" (two-bay front) x 47' (including flounder-roofed ell), two stories on raised basement, gable roof, semicircular fanlight above entrance, stone frame with impost blocks and keystone, splayed lintel-and-keystone motif on windows. Built c. 1815; demolished. 4 sheets (1936, including plans, elevations, details); 3 ext. photos (1936).

Walsh-McLean House (Indonesian Embassy) (DC-266), 2020 Massachusetts Ave., N.W. Brick with stone trim, approx. 95' square, undulating walls with rounded bays and corners, three-and-a-half stories with basement, tiled mansard roof with balustrade at eaves, large chimneys capped with segmental pediments, porte cochere to W., conservatory to E., lavish eclectic Beaux Art style; entertaining rooms on first floor, ballroom on top floor, central interior feature is three-story galleried stairwell with stained-glass skylight. Built 1901-3; Henry Anderson, architect. Builder was Thomas Walsh, Irish immigrant who struck it rich in Colorado gold fields; next owned by his daughter Evalyn Walsh McLean, socialite and last private owner of Hope Diamond; house renovated 1952 when became Indonesian Embassy. 2 ext. photos (1970*), 8 int. photos (1970*), photocopy of plan (1972*); 24 data pages (1970-73*). NR, JCL II

Warder Building (now Atlas Building) (DC-216), 527 9th St., N.W., SE. corner 9th and F Sts., N.W. Brick, 33'-5" (two bays) x 120'-4" (twelve bays), six stories, flat roof, lower two stories combined in arcaded treatment, string courses, windows doubly and triply grouped, patterned brick frieze, central elevator lobby and stair hall, sheet metal ceilings, molded wooden trim. Built c. 1890; first-story storefronts and interiors largely remodeled. 3 ext. photos (1969); 5 data pages (1969). NR, JCL II

Washington Club. See Patterson House (DC-269), 15 Dupont Circle, N.W.

Walsh-McLean House

Washington Hotel (DC-317), NE. corner 15th St. and
Pennsylvania Ave., N.W. Steel frame, smooth rusticated stone
veneer below third story, brick above with stone quoins,
fourteen-bay facade, six-bay and eleven-bay sides, nine stories
with four-bay tenth story and roof garden, bracketed cornice

above eighth floor, sgraffito decoration in spandrels and around 155
windows executed by Italian artists. Built 1917-18; Carrère and
Hastings, architects; partially remodeled 1968. Home of Vice
President John Nance Garner, Supreme Court Justice Frank
Murphy, and Speaker of the House John McCormick. 1 ext.
photo (1967*). JCL III

Washington Loan and Trust Company (now Riggs National
Bank, Washington Loan and Trust Branch) (DC-217), SW.
corner F and 9th Sts., N.W. Granite and brick, 122'-2" (ten-bay
front) x 116', nine stories, flat roof, facades divided horizontally into groups of stories by arcaded treatment, corbeled
string courses and cornice, U-shaped plan above first story,
exterior bearing wall construction, floors arched hollow tile on
steel joists, notable banking room with Roman Corinthian
columns. Built 1891; James G. Hill, architect; banking room
remodeled 1912; western addition 1926; Arthur Heaton,
architect; later interior modernization. 3 ext. photos (1969), 2
int. photos (1969); 8 data pages (1969). NR, JCL II

Washington Loan and Trust Company, West End Branch (Riggs
National Bank, 17th and G Street Branch) (DC-344), SW.
corner 17th and G Sts., N.W. Smooth-faced ashlar masonry,
approx. 100' (three-bay 17th St. facade), one story, flat tile
roof, bracketed pent eaves, facade has three arched openings
outlined by heavy rope molding, carved animal figures, masks
and heads decorate cornice, architraves and medallions, Italian
Renaissance style. Built 1924; Arthur Heaton, architect; demolished 1974. 5 ext. photos (1974*). JCL III

Washington Monument (DC-349), located on high ground W. of
15th St. between Independence and Constitution Aves., N.W.
White Maryland marble with granite backing, 555'-tall four-
sided obelisk topped by pyramidion with observation windows,
55' square at base, open central shaft contains cast-iron stairway
and passenger elevator, pyramidal capstone of solid aluminum
cast in 1884 (largest piece of cast aluminum to that date).
Original design by Robert Mills included circular rotunda with
peristyle of 30 columns at the base of 600' obelisk; present
proportions suggested by George Perkins Marsh, U.S. minister
to Italy. Construction began 1848, financed by public funds
raised by the Washington National Monument Society; work
virtually halted in 1855 after takeover of Monument Society by
the Know-Nothing political party ended public contributions;

monument stood as 176′ stump 1855-80; 13 courses of inferior marble laid by Know-Nothings removed in 1876 when responsibility for monument assumed by U.S. Army Corps of Engineers, Lt. Col. Thomas L. Casey, engineer in charge; original foundations enlarged 1879-80; shaft completed 1880-84; steam elevator installed 1886; electric elevator installed 1901. First administered by the Army Corps of Engineers; under jurisdiction of the National Park Service since 1933. 8 ext. photos (1971*). NPS, JCL I

Washington Navy Yard
  Commandant's House (Quarters A, Thomas Tingey House) (DC-12), E. of main gate of Washington Navy Yard at 8th and M Sts., S.E. Brick with Aquia stone trim, 48′-2″ (five-bay front) x 32′-2″ (three bays), two-and-a-half stories with basement, gable roof, three central bays form projecting pavilion with pediment, stone belt course, modillion cornice, entrance has semicircular fanlight and side lights, Palladian window above, splayed lintels with keystones, one-story porch along S. and E. sides, central hall plan. Built 1804; attributed to William Lovering; renovated mid 19th C. with new mantels, stairs, trim, windows lengthened. Home of first

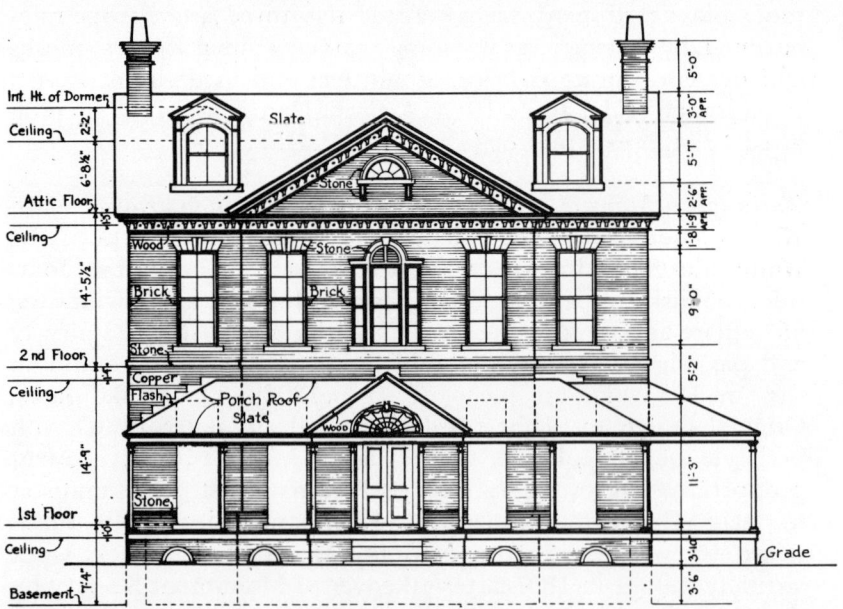

Washington Navy Yard, Commandant's House

Navy Yard commandant, Capt. Thomas Tingey, and all
subsequent commandants. 2 sheets (1936, including plan,
elevations, details), 7 sheets of unfinished drawings (1965*,
including plans, elevations); 7 ext. photos (1936, 1965), 2 int.
photos (1965); 9 data pages (1965). NR, JCL II

Main Gate (DC-100A), 8th and M Sts., S.E. Stuccoed brick,
N. facade has central vehicular door flanked by Doric columns
supporting a plain frieze, pedestrian doors on either side,
vehicular door on S. is a large semicircular arch which springs
from grade level. Built 1805-6; Benjamin H. Latrobe, architect; original hipped roof and parapet with eagle motif
removed 1880-81 when gate encased in large three-story
building. One of earliest Greek Revival structures in the
country. 4 ext. photos (1965), 3 photocopies of drawings
(1858, 1873, n.d., including plans, elevations, section); 4 data
pages (1966). NR, JCL II

Quarters B (Second Officer's Quarters) (DC-101A), Charles
Morris Ave., E. of Leutze Park in Washington Navy Yard,
entrance at 8th and M Sts., S.E. Brick, 76'-10" (ten-bay front)
x 24', two-and-a-half stories, gable roof, double wooden porch
along front, one room deep plan with entry to rooms from
rear hall. Built 1801; Lovering and Dyer, designer / builders;
southern five bays are original house; enlarged twice to
present size before 1868; two service wings to N. First
permanent structure built at Navy Yard. 8 sheets (1965,
including plans, elevations, details); 3 ext. photos (1965), 1
int. photo (1965), 4 photocopies of drawings (1868, n.d.); 4
data pages (1965). NR, JCL II

West Georgetown School (DC-110), 1640 Wisconsin Ave., N.W.
(Georgetown). Brick, irregular five-sided plan, 79'-1"(three-bay
east facade) x approx. 40' (north facade), two stories, low
hipped roof with pedimented central pavilion, recessed entrance
framed by Ionic pilasters and segmental pediment, modillion
cornice with dentil course, Georgian Revival details. Built 1911;
Snowdon Ashford, architect; interior extensively remodeled for
commercial use 1954-55; Deigert and Yerkes, architects. 5 ext.
photos (1966), 2 ext. photocopies (n.d.); 8 data pages (1966).

Westory Building (DC-329), 605 14th St., NE. corner 14th and
F Sts., N.W. Steel frame, brick and cast terra-cotta walls, seven
paired bays on front, two on flank, nine stories, flat roof,
boldly projecting cornice, rusticated columns on first two

floors, entablature above, elaborate terra-cotta ornament. Built 1906-8; Henry L. A. Jeckel, architect. 1 ext. photo (1967*).

West Washington Hotel (DC-103), 1238 Wisconsin Ave., N.W. (Georgetown). Brick, 30'-3" (four-bay front) x approx. 100' (including additions), four stories, flat roof with metal modillion cornice, tin lintels, shallow ornamental one-story wooden porch of same period, but not original to building. Built c. 1851; later rear additions; interior extensively altered. An important Washington hotel and meeting place during much of its existence. 2 ext. photos (1966); 7 data pages (1966).

Wheatley, Francis, House (DC-114), 3060-66 M St., N.W. (Georgetown). Brick double building with cast-iron shop fronts, each unit 17'-6" (front) x 90' (including rear ells), three stories, flat roof, heavy wooden cornice with paired brackets, pediment in center of each unit, brick hood molds, cornice above shop fronts supported by curvilinear cast-iron brackets. Built c. 1871; eastern shop front altered. 3 ext. photos (1966); 9 data pages (1966).

Wheatley Row House (DC-168), 1018 29th St., N.W. (Georgetown). Brick 12'-4" (two-bay front) x 28', two stories with basement fully exposed in rear, flat roof, wood and metal cornice, side hall plan. Built 1884-87; interior altered in 1946. Southernmost of eight identical row houses. 5 ext. photos (1967, including a view of entire row), photocopy of sketch plans (1967); 13 data pages (1967).

Wheatley Town House (DC-186), 3043 N St., N.W. (Georgetown). Brick row house, 22'-8" (three-bay front) x 35', three stories on raised basement, gable roof, bracketed modillion cornice, ornamental cast-iron window hoods, cast-iron balcony beneath first floor windows, pedimented door enframement with floral consoles, side hall plan, adjoins nearly identical house to east, good example of upper-class townhouse of mid 19th C. Built 1859 by Francis Wheatley; first floor kitchen addition in 20th C. 2 ext. photos (1968, 1969, one of adjoining house at 3041 N St.), 3 int. photos (1968), photocopy of sketch plan (1968); 11 data pages (1968).

Wheat Row (DC-10), 1315-21 4th St., S. W. Brick row houses, four units designed to appear as a single structure, 102' (twelve-bay front, each unit three bays) x 34', three stories, full

Wheatley Town House

basement with areaway on E., hipped roof, four-bay slightly
projecting central pavilion with pediment, belt courses between
floors, wooden fretwork cornice, entrance doors with semicircular fanlights, stone voussoir and keystones, side hall plans. Built
c. 1794; attributed to William Lovering, atchitect for the
Greenleaf Syndicate, which owned a third of the lots in early
Washington; rehabilitated 1964-65 as part of Harbour Square
urban renewal housing project. 5 sheets (1937, including plans,
elevation, details); 6 ext. photos (1936, 1937, 1971*), 1 int.
photo (1936). NR, JCL II.

White House, West Wing, The (DC-37), 1600 Pennsylvania Ave., N.W. Originally stuccoed ashlar, one-and-a-half stories with frieze windows, flat roof with balustrade, Classical Revival style, joined to main house by colonnade which incorporates part of Jefferson's 1807 terraces. Built 1902 to separate office functions from living quarters; McKim, Mead and White, architects; oval office added 1909; damaged by fire 1929; rebuilt and enlarged 1934-35. 3 ext. photos (1934, before alterations). NHL, JCL I (entire structure)

Wilkins House (formerly Australian Embassy, now Peruvian Embassy) (DC-276), 1700 Massachusetts Ave., N.W. Brick with limestone facing, horizontal rustication on ground floor, smooth-faced ashlar above, three part facade, 24'-6" (three-bay Massachusetts Ave. facade) x 39'-2" (three-bay diagonal entrance facade joining other two elevations) x 43' (three-bay 17th St. facade), four stories, flat roof, arched entrance with balcony above, Italian Renaissance Revival style, interior has English Jacobean motifs. Built 1909-10; J. H. de Sibour, architect; roof balustrade removed. 1 ext. photo (1970*), 6 int. photos (1970*), 1 ext. photocopy (c. 1915*), photocopy of drawing (1909*), photocopy of plan (1972*); 18 data pages (1970-73*), JCL III

Wilkins-Rogers Milling Company. See Bomford's Mill (DC-143), SW. corner of Potomac and Grace Sts., N.W. (Georgetown).

Willard Hotel (DC-293), NW. corner 14th St. and Pennsylvania Ave., N. W., running completely through block to F St., N. W. Steel frame, rusticated limestone facing on first three floors, light-colored brick above channeled to resemble the stone masonry below, 139' (seven-bay Pennsylvania Ave. facade) x 309' (sixteen bays), eleven stories plus additional story under large convex mansard roof, sloping site with only ten stories exposed on F St. facade, Pennsylvania Ave. entrance has monumental three-story Doric portico with balustrade and urn decorations, fifth-story windows have pediments and iron balconies, cornice above tenth floor supported by large ornamental consoles, large decorative dormers, turret at SE. corner, interior features lobby, public rooms, and promenade on first floor, ballroom in twelfth floor. Built 1900-1901; Henry J. Hardenbergh, architect; addition to F St. facade 1925; interiors altered. As one of the capital's premier hotels, this building and the old Willard previously on the site housed many notable

Willard Hotel

persons and was the scene of important events in the history of the country. 2 ext. photos (1967*, 1968*), 11 int. photos (1968*). NR, JCL II

Williams, John S., House (Decatur-Gunther House) (DC-29), 2812 N St., N. W. (Georgetown). Brick, approx. 80′ (three bays on street facade, four bays on garden facade), two-bay approx. 31′ addition to E., two-and-a-half stories on raised basement, gable roof (slightly lower on addition), elliptical-arched doorway with fanlight and side lights, flat lintels with corner blocks, balustraded porch across garden facade. Built 1813; traditionally associated with widow of Com. Stephen Decatur. 4 sheets (1937, including plans, elevations, details); 3 ext. photos (1935, 1942). JCL II

Williamson, William, House (DC-63), 2900 N St., N.W. (Georgetown). Brick, three-bay front, two-and-a-half stories on raised basement, gable roof, elliptical-arched entrance, fanlight and side lights with tracery. Built sometime between 1820 and 1830; first floor now has a single large Palladian window; side addition. 1 ext. photo (1942, doorway). JCL III

Wilson, Woodrow, House (Henry Parker Fairbanks House) (DC-133), 2340 S St., N.W. Historic house museum of the National Trust for Historic Preservation. Brick, three stories (two stories plus elevated terrace in rear), one-story entrance portico with cast-iron railing, three Palladian windows on second floor, brick parapet, semicircular bay on rear with door to terrace, Palladian-arched loggia opening onto roof of bay, Adamesque interiors, Georgian Revival style. Built 1915 for Henry Parker Fairbanks; Waddy B. Wood, architect. Home of Woodrow Wilson after he left the presidency. 3 ext. photos (1964*), 8 int. photos (1964*). NHL, JCL II

Wiltberger, Charles, House (John Maury House) (DC-4), 302 C St., N.W. Brick, 28'-2" (three-bay front) x 87' (including rear ell), two-and-a-half stories on full raised basement, gable roof, classical entrance enframement, straight transom with tracery, flat window lintels, bull's-eye corner blocks, curving granite stair with wrought-iron rail, double rear porch, side hall plan, double colonnettes flank entrance hall, round-ended room in ell, garden wall joins ell to stable. Built c. 1825; ell added c. 1836; demolished. Home of John Maury, early mayor of Washington. 5 sheets (1934, including plot plan, plans, elevations, sections, details); 1 int. photocopy (c. 1915); 2 data pages (1936).

Wisconsin Avenue Bridge. See High Street Bridge, (DC-30), Wisconsin Ave., N.W. over C. & O. Canal.

Woodley (Philip Barton Key House, now Maret School) (DC-52), 3000 Cathedral Ave., N.W. Stuccoed brick, three-story three-bay central block with two-story one-bay wings, low hipped roof, central balustraded deck, modillion cornice, wings have round ends in rear, one-story balustraded entrance portico with paired Ionic columns, small antechambers on either side, semicircular arched door with fanlight, wooden porch across rear, lower wing to E. Built 1806 by Philip Barton Key, lawyer, member of Congress from Maryland, and uncle of Francis Scott Key; interiors altered; classroom addition to E. of service wing. Served as summer retreat for President Cleveland; supposed to have been similarly used by Van Buren, Tyler, and Buchanan; also home of Col. Edward M. House, confidant of Woodrow Wilson and Henry L. Stimson, secretary of war and of state; became Maret School 1952. 3 ext. photos (1958), 3 int. photos (1958); 2 data pages (1959); HABSI form (1958). JCL II

Worthington House. See John Thomson Mason House (DC-167), 3425 Prospect St., N.W. (Georgetown).

Zepp Row House (DC-208), 1407 37th St., N.W. (Georgetown). One of nine brick row houses, 16' (three-bay front) x 30', two stories, flat roof with pent eave across front, unornamented facade, side hall plan. Built 1916 as speculative housing by contractor Guy S. Zepp. 2 ext. photos (1968*); 21 data pages (1968*).

APPENDIXES
INDEX

Appendix 1

Buildings Arranged by Street Address

A

Adams Mill Rd., N.W., N. of Ontario Pl. See Jackson Hill

B

Bladensburg Rd. at New York Ave., N.E. See Anton Ruppert House

C

302 C St., N.W. See Charles Wiltberger House
C & O Canal, N. bank. See Godey Lime Kilns
Canal Rd. at Reservoir Rd., N.W. See Abner Cloud House
Canal St., S.E. See Southeast Neighborhood Area Study (DC-71)
Carroll St., S.E. See Southeast Neighborhood Area Study (DC-71)
3000 Cathedral Ave., N.W. See Woodley
Connecticut Ave., N.W., opposite entrance to National Zoological Park. See Oak Hill
Constitution Ave., N.W. between 7th and 8th Sts. See National Archives
Constitution Ave., N.W. at 7th and 15th Sts. See U.S. Capitol Gateposts
Constitution Ave., N.W. at 15th and 17th Sts. See U.S. Capitol Gatehouses
Constitution Ave., N.W. at 17th St., SW. corner. See Lock Keeper's House
Constitution Ave., N.W. between 17th and 21st Sts. See U.S. Navy and Munitions Building
1301 Corcoran St., N.W. See Zalmon Richards House

D

629 D St., N.W. See Commercial Building
1776 D St., N.W. See Memorial Continental Hall
2600 Block of D St., N.W. See Easby House
22 D St., S.E. See House
3015 Dumbarton Ave., N.W. (Georgetown). See House
3123 Dumbarton Ave., N.W. (Georgetown). See Foxhall-McKenney House
15 Dupont Circle, N.W. See Patterson House

514 E St., N.W. See House
625 E St., N.W. See Building
809 E St., N.W. See Frederick B. Culver House
E and 14th Sts., N.W., SE. corner. See District Building
2029 E St., N.W. See House
200 East Capitol St., N.E. See Edwin C. Manning House
500 East Capitol St., N.E. See House

F

F St., N.W., between 7th and 8th Sts. See U.S. General Post
    Office
800-812 F St., N.W. See LeDroit Building
814 F St., N.W. See Commercial Building
816 F St., N.W. See Adams Building
818 F St., N.W. See Commercial Building
F St., N.W., between 7th, 9th, and G Sts. See Patent Office
    Building
F and 9th Sts., N.W., SW. corner. See Washington Loan and
    Trust Co.
F and 9th Sts., N.W., NW. corner. See Masonic Temple
1315-17 F St., N.W. See American Bank Building
1427 F St., N.W. See Commercial Building
F St., N.W., between 17th and 18th Sts. See Michler Place
1901 F St., N.W. See Row House
1903-11 F St., N.W. See Row Houses
1925 F St., N.W. See Alexander Ray House
Florida and Rhode Island Aves., N.W. See LeDroit Park

G

G St., N.W., between 4th, 5th, and F Sts. See Pension Building
G St., N.W., between 12th and 13th Sts. See Commercial
    Buildings
G St., S.E. See Southeast Neighborhood Area Study (DC-73)
620 G St., S.E. See Christ Church
801 G St., S.E. See U.S. Marine Corps Commandant's House
601 G St., S.W. See House
613-31 G St., S.W. See Row Houses
5760 Georgia Ave., N.W. See District of Columbia Engine Co.
    No. 22 Firehouse

1003 H St., N.W. See House

H St. and Madison Pl., N.W., SE. corner. See Richard Cutts House

Hillyer Place, N.W. See Hillyer Place

607 Howard Pl., N.W. See Gen. Oliver O. Howard House

I

1500 I St., N.W. See John R. McLean House

1600 I St., N.W. See Tuckerman House

1601 I St., N.W. See Horace Gray House

I St., N.W. between 18th and 19th Sts. See House

I St., N.W. at 20th St. See House

2017 I St., N.W. See Timothy Caldwell House

I St., S.E. See Southeast Neighborhood Area Study (DC-73)

1000-1002 Independence Ave., S.W. See Houses

451 Indiana Ave., N.W. See District of Columbia City Hall

625 Indiana Ave., N.W. See Commercial Building

J

748 Jackson Pl., N.W. See Decatur House

Jefferson Dr., S.W., between 9th and 12th Sts. See Smithsonian Institution Building

900 Jefferson Dr., S.W. See Smithsonian Institution, Arts and Industries Building

K

1643 K St., N.W. See District of Columbia Engine Co. No. 1 Firehouse

2618-20 K St., N.W. See Robert Peter Houses

3142 K St., N.W. (Georgetown). See Capital Traction Co. Powerhouse

3260-62 K St., N.W. (Georgetown). See Ray's Warehouse and Office

K St., S.E. See Southeast Neighborhood Area Study (DC-73)

2401 Kalorama Rd., N.W. See The Lindens

L

1011 L St., N.W. See Chinese Community Church

L St., S.E. See Southeast Neighborhood Area Study (DC-73)

Massachusetts Ave., Louisana Ave., and 1st St., N.E. See Union
   Station
438 Massachusetts Ave., N.W. See District of Columbia Engine
   Co. No. 6 Firehouse
1700 Massachusetts Ave., N.W. See Wilkins House
1746 Massachusetts Ave., N.W. See Clarence Moore House
1785 Massachusetts Ave., N.W. See McCormick Apartments
1801 Massachusetts Ave., N.W. See Herbert Wadsworth House
2010 Massachusetts Ave., N.W. See Grace Denio Litchfield
   House
2020 Massachusetts Ave., N.W. See Walsh-McLean House
2118 Massachusetts Ave., N.W. See Larz Anderson House
2121 Massachusetts Ave., N.W. See Townsend House
2200 Massachusetts Ave., N.W. See Alexander Stewart House
2201 Massachusetts Ave., N.W. See Miller House
2230 Massachusetts Ave., N.W. See James C. Hooe House
2234 Massachusetts Ave., N.W. See Henrietta Halliday House
2301 Massachusetts Ave., N.W. See Joseph Beale House
2306 Massachusetts Ave., N.W. See Alice P. Barney Studio
2311 Massachusetts Ave., N.W. See Gibson Fahnestock House
2315 Massachusetts Ave., N.W. See Francis B. Moran House
2349 Massachusetts Ave., N.W. See Christian Hauge House
2370 Massachusetts Ave., N.W. See Arthur C. Stanley House
2516 Massachusetts Ave., N.W. See Japanese Embassy
2551 Massachusetts Ave., N.W. See Mosque
1227 Monroe St., N.E. See District of Columbia Engine Co. No.
   17 Firehouse

N

2806 N St., N.W. (Georgetown). See Isaac Owens House
2808 N St., N.W. (Georgetown). See John Stoddert Haw House
2817 N St., N.W. (Georgetown). See House
2900 N St., N.W. (Georgetown). See William Williamson House
3038 N St., N.W. (Georgetown). See Riggs-Riley House
3043 N St., N.W. (Georgetown). See Wheatley Town House
3233 N St., N.W. (Georgetown). See Gazebo
3255-63 N St., N.W. (Georgetown). See Smith Row
3339 N St., N.W. (Georgetown). See Col. John Cox House
3606 N St., N.W. (Georgetown). See Findley House
456 N St., S.W. See Edward Simon Lewis House
468-70 N St., S.W. See Duncanson-Cranch House
1307 New Hampshire Ave., N.W. See Christian Heurich Mansion
1320 New York Ave., N.W. See Capital Garage
1729 New York Ave., N.W. See Lemon Building

Pennsylvania Ave., N.W., between 11th and 12th Sts. See U.S.
Post Office Department

1201 Pennsylvania Ave., N.W. See Commercial Building

1347 Pennsylvania Ave., N.W. See Commercial Building

Pennsylvania Ave. and 14th St., N.W., NW. corner. See Willard
Hotel

1411-13 Pennsylvania Ave., N.W. See Occidental Hotel and
Restaurant

1500 Pennsylvania Ave., N.W. See U.S. Treasury Department

1600 Pennsylvania Ave., N.W. See White House, West Wing

1651 Pennsylvania Ave., N.W. See Joseph Lovell House

Pennsylvania Ave. and 17th St., N.W., NE. corner. See Corcoran
Gallery of Art

Pennsylvania Ave. and 17th St., N.W., SE. corner. See State,
War, and Navy Building

Pennsylvania Ave. and 18th St., N.W., NE. corner. See
Powhatan Hotel

1901-13 Pennsylvania Ave., N.W. See Seven Buildings

1922-32 Pennsylvania Ave., N.W. See Commercial Buildings

2411 Pennsylvania Ave., N.W. See House

206 Pennsylvania Ave., S.E. See Elias Caldwell House

1830 Phelps Pl., N.W. See Bebb House

1052-54 Potomac St., N.W. (Georgetown). See Joseph Carleton
House

1061-63 Potomac St., N.W. (Georgetown). See Double House

Potomac and Grace Sts., N.W., SW. corner (Georgetown). See
Bomford's Mill

Potomac St., S.E. See Southeast Neighborhood Area Study
(DC-71)

3400 Prospect St., N.W. (Georgetown). See Halcyon House

3425 Prospect St., N.W. (Georgetown). See John Thomson
Mason House

3508 Prospect St., N.W. (Georgetown). See Prospect House

3617-21 Prospect St., N.W. (Georgetown). See Harnedy Row
Houses

Q

1615 Q St., N.W. See Cairo Hotel

1700 Block of Q St., N.W. See Row Houses

2715 Q St., N.W. (Georgetown). See Dumbarton House

3013 Q St., N.W. (Georgetown). See Cooke's Row, Villa No. 3

3099 Q St., N.W. (Georgetown). See W. Taylor Birch House

3124 Q St., N.W. (Georgetown). See Bowie-Sevier House

R

931 R St., N.W. See District of Columbia Engine Co. No. 4 Firehouse

2223 R St., N.W. See Charles Evans Hughes House

2253 R St., N.W. See Emma S. Fitzhugh House

3001 R St., N.W. (Georgetown). See Oak Hill Cemetery Chapel and Gatehouse

R St. at Avon Pl., N.W. (Georgetown). See Jackson School

4437 Reservoir Rd., N.W. See House

Rock Creek Cemetery. See Adams Memorial and St. Paul's Church

Rock Creek Church Rd. and Upshur St., N.W. See U.S. Soldiers Home

Rock Creek Park, N. of Calvert St. Bridge. See Estes Mill Ruins

S

2340 S St., N.W. See Woodrow Wilson House

3134 South St., N.W. (Georgetown). See Brickyard Hill House

630 South Carolina Ave., S.E. See The Maples

T

49 T St., S.W. See Capt. Joseph Johnson House

Theodore Roosevelt Island. See John Mason House

1058 Thomas Jefferson St., N.W. (Georgetown). See Potomac Lodge No. 5

1063 Thomas Jefferson St., N.W. (Georgetown). See House

1069 Thomas Jefferson St., N.W. (Georgetown). See Nicholas Hedges House

1072 Thomas Jefferson St., N.W. (Georgetown). See Adams-Mason House

Tilden St., N.W. at Beach Dr., NW. corner. See Peirce Mill

U

1624 U St., N.W. See District of Cloumbia Engine Co. No. 9 Firehouse

V

1345 V St., S.E. See District of Columbia Engine Co. No. 15 Firehouse

Vermont and Rhode Island Aves., N.W. See Logan Circle

1239 Vermont Ave., N.W. See Gen. Montgomery C. Meigs House

W

1411 W St., S.E. See Frederick Douglass House

3545 Williamsburg Ln., N.W. See Linnean Hill

1006 Wisconsin Ave., N.W. (Georgetown). See Francis Dodge
    Warehouse

1041 Wisconsin Ave., N.W, (Georgetown). See Grace Church

Wisconsin Ave., N.W. at C & O Canal. See High Street Bridge

1066 Wisconsin Ave., N.W. (Georgetown). See Vigilant Fire-
    house

1200 Wisconsin Ave., N.W. (Georgetown). See Potomac Savings
    Bank

1220 Wisconsin Ave., N.W. (Georgetown). See John Davidson
    House

1238 Wisconsin Ave., N.W. (Georgetown). See West Washington
    Hotel

1254 Wisconsin Ave., N.W. (Georgetown). See Stohlman's
    Confectionary

1255 Wisconsin Ave., N.W. (Georgetown). See John Lutz House

1321½–1325½ Wisconsin Ave., N.W. (Georgetown). See
    Marcey-Payne Building

1335 Wisconsin Ave., N.W. (Georgetown). See William
    Marceron Building

1522 Wisconsin Ave., N W. (Georgetown). See Beall's Express
    Building

1527-29 Wisconsin Ave., N.W. (Georgetown). See House

1530 Wisconsin Ave., N.W. (Georgetown). See House

1640 Wisconsin Ave., N.W. (Georgetown). See West George-
    town School

1

1st and East Capitol Sts., N.E. corner. See U.S. Supreme Court
    Building

1st St., S.E. at Independence Ave. See Library of Congress

1st St., S.E. See Southeast Neighborhood Area Study (DC-74)

2

2d St., S.E. See Southeast Neighborhood Area Study (DC-74)

2d, E, and F Sts. and New Jersey Ave., S.E. See Duddington

3d and G Sts., N.W., NE. corner. See Adas Israel Synagogue

4

1315-21 4th St., S.W. See Wheat Row

6

507 6th St., N.W. See Apartment Building
513 6th St., N.W. See House
6th and G Sts., N.W. See Adas Israel Synagogue
6th St., S.E. See Southeast Neighborhood Area Study (DC-74)
711 6th St., S.E. See Isaac Pierce House
601-13 6th St., S.W. See Row Houses
1252 6th St., S.W. See Thomas Law House

7

7th St. and Florida Ave., N.E. See Gallaudet College, Chapel
Hall, College Hall, and President's House
301 7th St., N.W. See National Bank of Washington
303 7th St., N.W. See Firemen's Insurance Co. Building
400 7th St., N.W. See Commercial Building
401-7 7th St., N.W. See Germond Crandell Building
415 7th St., N.W. See Commercial Building
7th and F Sts., N.W. See Commercial Buildings
7th and G Sts., N.W., NW. corner. See Merchants and Mechanics
Savings Bank
7th St., S.E. See Southeast Neighborhood Area Study (DC-74)
7th St., S.E. Between C St. and North Carolina Ave. See Eastern
Market
7th St. and Independence Ave., S.W., SW. corner. See Army
Medical Museum and Library

8

308-10 8th St., N.W. See Commercial Buildings
320 8th St., N.W. See House
1515 8th St., N.W. See Immaculate Conception Church
8th and M Sts., S.E. See Washington Navy Yard, Commandant's
House, Main Gate, and Quarters B

9

527 9th St., N.W. See Warder Building
616 9th St., N.W. See Commercial Building

618 9th St., N.W. See Commercial Building
918 9th St., N.W. See Mount Vernon Theater
9th St., S.E. See Southeast Neighborhood Area Study (DC-74)

10

418 10th St., N.W. See United States Storage Co.
511 10th St., N.W. See Ford's Theater
516 10th St., N.W. See Petersen House
10th St., S.E. See Southeast Neighborhood Area Study (DC-74)

11

1633 11th St., N.W. See Scottish Rite Temple
11th St., S.E. See Southeast Neighborhood Area Study (DC-74)
304-6 11th St., S.W. See Double House and Stable

12

719 12th St., N.W. See District of Columbia Engine Co. No. 2
Firehouse

13

13th and K Sts., N.W., SE. corner. See Franklin School

14

605 14th St., N.W. See Westory Building

15

15th St. and Benning Rd., N.E. See Columbia Railway Co. Car
Barns
15th St., N.W. between Independence and Constitution Aves.
See Washington Monument
15th St. and Pennsylvania Ave., N.W., NE. corner. See
Washington Hotel
601-3 15th St., N.W. See Rhodes Tavern

16

16th and H Sts., N.W., NE. corner. See St. John's Church
1119-25 16th St., N.W. See Pullman House

17

17th and E Sts., N.W., SW. corner. See Red Cross
528 17th St., N.W. See Josiah King House

17th and G Sts., N.W., SW. corner. See Washington Loan and Trust Co., West End Branch

18

18th and N Sts., N.W., SE. corner. See Church of the Covenant

19

19th and I Sts., N.W., SW. corner. See Nineteenth Street Baptist Church

20

412 20th St., N.W. See Hamburgh Village House
723-25 20th St., N.W. See House
20th and R Sts., N.W., NE. corner. See George Fraser House

23

23d and E Sts., N.W. See Naval Observatory, Old
1606 23d St., N.W. See Edward H. Everett House

24

2000 24th St., N.W. See Devore-Chase House

26

26th St., N.W. and Pennsylvania Ave. See Humble Service Station

27

932 27th St., N.W. See David Walker House
27th and Dumbarton Ave., N.W., SE. corner (Georgetown). See First Baptist Church of Georgetown

28

1221 28th St., N.W. (Georgetown). See Methodist Episcopal Parsonage House
1222 28th St., N.W. (Georgetown). See Cottage
1524 28th St., N.W. (Georgetown). See Benjamin Miller House
1534 28th St., N.W. (Georgetown). See Robert Dodge House
1623 28th St., N.W. (Georgetown). See Evermay

1018 29th St., N.W. (Georgetown). See Wheatley Row House

1400 29th St., N.W. (Georgetown). See James I. Barrett House

1334 29th St., N.W. (Georgetown). See Mt. Zion United Methodist Church

1633 29th St., N.W. (Georgetown). See Mackall Square

30

1050 30th St., N.W. (Georgetown). See Duvall Foundry

1060 30th St., N.W. (Georgetown). See McCleery House

1208 30th St., N.W. (Georgetown). See Andrew Ross Tenant House 1

1210 30th St., N.W. (Georgetown). See Andrew Ross Tenant House II

1228 30th St., N.W. (Georgetown). See William Knowles House

1241 30th St., N.W. (Georgetown). See Edgar Patterson House

1314 30th St., N.W. (Georgetown). See Grafton Tyler Double House

1320 30th St., N.W. (Georgetown). See De La Roche-Jewell Tenant House

2618 30th St., N.W. See House

31

1313 31st St., N.W. (Georgetown). See Carriage House

1402 31st St., N.W. (Georgetown). See Philip T. Berry House

1644 31st St., N.W. (Georgetown). See Tudor Place

1694 31st St., N.W. (Georgetown). See Albert Jackson House

35

1306 35th St., N.W. (Georgetown). See Carroll Daly House

1307 35th St., N.W. (Georgetown). See Goszler-Manogue House

1311 35th St., N.W. (Georgetown). See Bussard-Newman House

1331 35th St., N.W. (Georgetown). See Jeremiah Sullivan Building

1404 35th St., N.W. (Georgetown). See Brown House

1408 35th St., N.W. (Georgetown). See Bronaugh-Bibb-Libby House

1411 35th St., N.W. (Georgetown). See William Mankins House

1500 35th St., N.W. (Georgetown). See Georgetown Visitation Convent

1503 35th St., N.W. (Georgetown). See Herron-Moxley House
1537 35th St., N.W. (Georgetown). See Volta Bureau
1555 35th St., N.W. (Georgetown). See Longden House

36

36th St., N.W. (extended) at Potomac River. See Potomac
Aqueduct
36th St., N.W. between N and O Sts. (Georgetown). See Holy
Trinity Parish
1419 36th St., N.W. (Georgetown). See Daniel Kane House
1423 36th St., N.W. (Georgetown). See Mahorney-Harrington
House

37

1239 37th St., N.W. (Georgetown). See Kelly House
1407 37th St., N.W. (Georgetown). See Zepp Row House
37th and O Sts., N.W. (Georgetown). See Georgetown University, Healy Building, and Old North Building

Appendix 2

Buildings Recorded on Historic American Buildings Survey Inventory Forms

The following buildings were recorded on the one-page inventory forms in use from 1953 to 1970. The forms are filed in the Prints and Photographs Division of the Library of Congress where they form a companion collection to the Historic American Buildings Survey. Those buildings marked with a † are more fully documented in the HABS archives and can be found listed in the main body of this catalog.

†Bank of Columbia, 3210 M St., N.W. (Georgetown)

Cherryhill Row Houses, 1021-43 Cecil Pl. and 1031-37 and 3203-21 Cherryhill Ln., N.W. (Georgetown)

Commercial Building, 609 C St., N.W.

Commercial Building, 620 C St., N.W. (rear of 621 Pennsylvania Ave., N.W.)

Commercial Building, 637 Indiana Ave., N.W.

Commercial Building, 639 Indiana Ave., N.W.

Commercial Building, 641 Indiana Ave., N.W.

†Corcoran Gallery of Art (Renwick Gallery), NE. corner Pennsylvania Ave. and 17th St., N.W.

†Cutts, Richard, House (Dolly Madison House), SE. corner H St. and Madison Pl., N.W.

†Forrest-Marbury House, 3350 M St., N.W. (Georgetown)

†Halcyon House (Benjamin Stoddert House), 3400 Prospect St., N.W. (Georgetown)

Highlands, The (Maj. Charles Joseph Nourse House), 3825 Wisconsin Ave., N.W.

†House, 1063 Thomas Jefferson St., N.W. (Georgetown)

†King, Josiah W., House (Samuel McKean House), 528 17th St., N.W.

Libby Row Houses, 1021-37 30th St., N.W. (Georgetown)

Loughborough House, 3041 M St., N.W. (Georgetown)

McGowan and Shinn Row Houses, 1058-66 30th St., N.W.(Georgetown)

†Meigs, Gen. Mongomery C., House, 1239 Vermont Ave., N.W.

Monroe, Thomas, House, 208 8th St., S.W.

†Patent Office Building, bounded by 7th, 9th, F, and G Sts., N.W.

†Peter, Robert, Houses, 2618-20 K St., N.W.

Index

This index is intended to supplement the alphabetically arranged catalog. Since buildings are listed in the catalog by proper name and are appropriately cross-referenced, building names have not been repeated in this index unless the building is discussed in the introduction or referred to in the entry for another building. When looking for information on a specific building, refer first to the catalog entries.

Credits